LETTERS FROM A RELIGIOS NUT

AN UNINTENDED good STORY

Stephanie Maier

ISBN (Paperback): 978-0-578-74921-1

Library of Congress Control Number: on file

Any references to real people, living or dead, have been marked out to protect privacy.

Front cover illustration by Stephanie Maier

First printing edition 2020

Podunk Press
9400 S Ocean Dr. #805B
Jensen Beach, FL 34957

www.FreedomDiner.us

For more books, products,
courses & other cool stuff

by Stephanie Maier

visit:

www.FreedomDiner.us

For God, who has the ultimate
sense of humor.

"Common sense and a sense of humor are the same thing, moving at different speeds. A sense of humor is just common sense, dancing."

--William James

Contents

Why this book, now?
xv

1
Can a woman become a Jedi Knight?
1

2
Can Baptists get into Purgatory?
6

3
Can I be a juggling nun?
10

4
Can I be a part-time nun?
13

5
Can I bring a Confessional to my hotel room?
23

6
Can I bring a case of Holy Water on the plane?
30

7

Can I bring my cockatoo to mass?

32

8

Can I buy your church's Confessional?

36

9

Can I shine the shoes outside of your mosque?

40

10

Can I wear my burqa to exercise class?

43

11

Can I wear my nun's habit skydiving?

53

12

Can my husband's prize pig be buried next to him?

61

13

Can my nephew rap the Torah at his Bar Mitzvah?

66

14

Can my Sheiks bring their prayer mats to your gym?

73

15
Can you Baptize my dog?
76

16
Can you Bar Mitzvah my dog?
83

17
Can you circumcise my dog?
85

18
Can you flavor the Communion wafers?
91

19
Can you make a Confession booth for me?
94

20
Can you make a religious soup?
97

21
Can you make a sexy Muslim tv show?
101

22
Can you make bottled Holy Water?
103

23
Can you make a Holy Goldfish cracker?
111

24
Can you make separate gender lines at my bank?
113

25
Can you paint me as Henry VIII?
117

26
Can you please find my Burqa?
123

27
Can you sage my hotel room for Indian spirits?
126

28
Can you stock my room with bottled Holy water?
137

29
Can you teach our nuns ballet?
142

30
Can your temple adopt my cows?
144

31
Do you bless your hot dogs by a Rabbi?
154

32
Does God have a sense of humor?
158

33
Help I think my dog is homosexual...
162

34
I left my Buddah in your taxi...
168

35
I left my Hatian Cleansing Kit in your hotel...
171

36
I need 200 Jewish mannequins...
176

37
If we become Scientologists, will we meet celebrities?
178

38
I'm coming to church and I have gas...
183

39
I'm coming to church and I look just like George W. Bush…
187

40
I'm coming to church with my guide horse…
191

41
I'm pleased to speak at your University…
199

42
When my husband dies, can I have my kidney back?
203

43
Where are all the Jewish mannequins?
206

44
Your Noni juice gives me healing powers…
213

Why this book, now?

Americans have lived in a divided house for some time, squabbling our way through 24 decades of evolution without ever really knowing the answer to the great chicken-and-egg question: Does our culture mirror societal values or do our values reflect our culture? As a child of the '70's, I shake my head curiously at today's controversies and wonder, "What would George and Archie have to say about it?" We could really use them right now.

Everyone's gotten so damn serious, walking around with a bloated sense of self-importance and moral superiority, lecturing the rest of us on how to live. Even twenty-somethings, who used to have *fun* before selling out to the nuclear joys of marriage, mortgages and middle-management have become chai-drinking "global citizens" with a dogmatic activism and Victorian-era-sensibility at the slightest social infraction, like some freakish-super-baby between Emily Post and Lord Baelish. And it's not even their fault: Their brains were given a thorough cleansing by rich, Marxist professors at those ivy-covered-North-Koreas we call college. The laser-like focus they demonstrate when instituting their endless rules, micro-aggressions and addiction for sorting everyone into oppressive categories is formidable. Having been properly labeled, they then send you down the social-justice assembly line as the 24-hour group-think-media slowly drains your soul from your body like some kind of politically-correct succubus.

Simply put: I couldn't send these emails today.

Letters from a Religious Nut started out as a joke. It was 2011. The p.c.-police were already out in force, so asking ridiculous religious questions to random strangers seemed like a good way to let off some steam. Historically, religion and politics were the two topics never to be discussed among members of polite society. The weather was traditionally considered the best option for cordial conversation, especially for women. So the irony isn't lost on me that I chose to spend my career engaged in vigorous political – and sometimes religious – discourse. And particularly *because* religion is such a hot-button topic, it seemed like the perfect one to push to try and shake people out of the oppressive seriousness that was weighing down on American society. By 2011, we had already reached that point where everybody just needed to lighten the hell up and this book was my, "In case of emergency, break glass" offering. No question and no one was off-limits: I queried pastors, rabbis, priests,vice presidents of department stores, and aerobics instructors. I asked questions related to every major religion and even a few fictional ones. Since my motive was self-serving, I wasn't concerned with a reply beyond the entertainment value there was in receiving one at all, most likely one telling me that I was an idiot.

The reality, however, was something quite different. Something remarkable. I wrote my stupid emails, and as the replies started rolling in, humanity found its voice. The vast majority of people were polite, patient, and even *helpful*. The more ludicrous my requests, the more people seemed willing to go through a pretty decent amount of inconvenience to accommodate me. *Why?* Could it be that people were - *good?* I saw little evidence on my television, the news, or social media, but it seemed to be true. And what began as a joke wound up reinvigorating my faith in the human spirit. The truth is that most people *are* good, and most want to see the same in others.

People were in fact so accommodating that I began to feel guilty exploiting their good-nature and had to devise fake reasons why I actually would *not* be coming to their church with my guide-pony "Daisy" or why, after their unexpected and enthusiastic, "Yes," I would in fact *not* be needing to have my own confession booth installed in my hotel room.

Now I look back through the lens of 2020 and see that the p.c.-police were in their infancy stages compared to where they are now. Today the vigilant flock from the Church of Social Justice has their tentacles in everything, even humor. And precisely *because* of that, we need this book now more than ever. We need to be ridiculous, silly, idiotic. What with the mask-Nazis, contact-tracing apps and social distancing mores, couldn't we all use a little silliness?

Yes, it's time to take this book off the shelf and send it out into the world. Every one of these emails was sent to a real person and every response is from a genuine, actual human being. The dates, times, text, and company names and job titles are all original; only the recipient names have been marked out for privacy reasons (and because I can't afford the lawsuits). I used many pseudonyms to suit whatever character I was intending to portray

in the email: faith5239@gmail.com is, I dare
say, still active.

So sit down with your favorite beverage, read
these emails, have a laugh, and for just
a moment, see the possibility that things
actually can be good again, because people
are good. For just a time, forget about the
media, the arguments, the social conventions,
the rules, and just be stupid. God knows we
need it.

Remember: Teacher says, every time a bell
rings, an angel identifies as a unicorn. And
that's okay.
                -- Stephanie Maier, July 4, 2020

1

On Sat, Apr 23, 2011 at 3:53 PM,
Stacey Brown <faith5239@gmail.com> wrote:

This is an enquiry e-mail via
http://templeofthejediorder.org
from: Stacey Brown <faith5239@gmail.com>

Dear Br. Xxxxxx,

I just discovered the existence of your Temple
a few months ago, and when I read about the
philosophy of the Jedi Knights, I knew I'd
found my home! It's true I'm a huge fan of
the Star Wars films, but you guys seem to
have taken this to a whole, new level. I want
to begin training, but I have some questions
that I couldn't find on the website. First,
can a woman become a Jedi Knight? If not,

1

what role can a woman serve in this religion? Even though your organization is not simply role playing but is living an entire belief system, do we also get to wear cool cloaks or anything? How about what women wear? And finally, I'm getting married in six months. Is there a Jedi wedding ceremony and if so, what does it entail?

Thanks very much for the information. I can't wait to hear back and get started!

May the force be with you,
Stacey Brown

On Sat, Apr 23, 2011 at 7:20 PM,
Xxxx Xxxxx Xxxxxx
<xxxx.xxxxx.xxxxxx@gmail.com> wrote:

We have female Knights, Masters, Ministers
and Bishops ... there is no discrimination at
all. If you are interested in becoming clergy
you attend our online Seminary.

We do use the Jedi style robes or cloaks for
formal and clerical wear.

There are a variety of Jedi ceremonies for
weddings. This depends on what you want and
what family and guests fell comfortable with.
I've known of some where the entire wedding
party was in full Star Wars costumes with
FX Lightsabers or where people wore ordinary
suits and the Jedi minister wore and ordinary
Jedi robe.

You can get some ideas from this book. It's not
proofread for publication but if you overlook
some spelling errors etc there's plenty of
information.

We can issue a Commission so that a friend
or relative can conduct the ceremony for you
as your minister without them having to go

through the training to become a licensed minister. This is a special Commission for a particular event that allows one to conduct a specific ceremony authorized by The Order when a Jedi Minister is not available.

Much of the site is not visible unless you are logged in due to copyright reasons and privacy. After you login read all the way down the front page and you'll see the Initiates Training Program.

You can get live help with the shoutbox and chat too.

MTFBWY,

Br. Xxxx+
Chaplain
Temple Of The Jedi Order

From: faith5239 <faith5239@gmail.com>

Subject: Re: Temple Of The Jedi Order:
new member questions

Date: April 25, 2011 at 10:10:46 AM EDT

To: Xxxx Xxxxx Xxxxxx
<xxxx.xxxxx.xxxxxx@gmail.com>

Dear Br. Xxxx,

Thank you very much for the information. I'm
going to study more and will be in touch when
I'm ready.

MTFBWY,
Stacey

2

From: faith5239 <faith5239@gmail.com>

Subject: Need help and have a suggestion

Date: May 10, 2011 at 3:33:12 PM EDT

To: xxxxxxxx@firstorlando.com

Dear Pastor Xxxxx,

I'm a regular at your church and consider myself a member. I come to the 10:45 service because I like the music so much. GREAT MUSIC, VERY INSPIRING!!

I'm writing because I need help with something, and I'm also making a suggestion for the betterment of Baptists everywhere.

The thing is, I'm not perfect, as no Christian is, and Baptists don't have Confession, so there's not much chance to make up for our sins besides just asking the Lord for forgiveness and hoping for the best. I figure with my record, I'm not a top candidate for Heaven but I'm also not nearly bad enough to go to Hell. This makes me an ideal candidate for Purgatory, except we don't have Purgatory. So I need to know: as a Baptist, how can I get into Purgatory? As I understand it, Purgatory is a step toward Heaven, kind of like a waiting room, until you're good enough to get a promotion. I really need this! So can you please help me? How do non-Catholics get into Purgatory?

Even better would be if you could use your connections with other Baptist Pastors to get us Purgatory. Maybe you guys have to sign a petition or something?

Thank you for this help; there's really nothing more important than the afterlife, and I want to plan ahead as best as I can. I really look forward to hearing from you soon.

Hoping to make it to God's Waiting Room,
Ryan

From: Xxxxx Xxx <Xxxxxxxx@FirstOrlando.com>

Subject: RE: Need help and have a suggestion

Date: May 11, 2011 at 10:07:41 AM EDT

To: 'faith5239' <faith5239@gmail.com>

Dear Ryan,

I'm so glad that you e-mailed me with your concern and questions.

Jesus died on the cross for us. Once we accept Jesus as our Lord and Savior, we know that heaven is our final destination.

John 3:16 says: For God so loved the world that He gave His only Son, that whosoever believes in Him should not perish but have everlasting life.

We do not have Purgatory. Our step to heaven is through Jesus.

I would really like for you to see a pastor when you come to church on Saturday night and he can sit down and talk with you one-on-one and personally answer your questions.

If you don't want to wait until Saturday night, come to church tonight. We serve dinner from 4:45 - 6:30pm for $6.00, and have a special church service tonight at 7pm. I would be glad to set you up with an appointment with one of our pastors if you can come tonight. Just let me know.

If you want to see me, it will take several weeks because my schedule is full, so I hope you are open to seeing another pastor. Let me know.
God's abundant blessings on you.

Under His wings,
Pastor Xxxxx

Dr. Xxxxx Xxx
Sr. Pastor
xxxx S. John Young Parkway
Orlando, Florida 32805

3

From: faith5239 <faith5239@gmail.com>

Subject: Important question about the calling

Date: March 17, 2011 at 8:10:42 PM EDT

To: vocations@carmelitedcj.org

Dear Carmelite Sisters of the Divine Heart of Jesus,

I'm twenty-two and a life-long Catholic. I love the Lord more than anything in this entire world, and I live my life for serving Him. I have long considered a life dedicated to God as a nun, and I really think that's where I want my life to be. I also, however, have a serious love for juggling. I'm actually a Master Juggler, trained at the Illinois

Juggling Institute in Bollingbrook, and I've since continued my juggling education through their website seminars. My love for juggling and my love for the Lord have been a very good match so far. I've used my gift to entertain children recovering in hospitals and they just love it!

In order for me to fulfill both dreams of my life, is it possible to become a part-time nun? I promise I would keep all of my vows! If being a part-time nun isn't offered, then is there such a thing as a juggling nun? Could I be a juggler and also a nun? Perhaps in that way, I could live as a nun but also help sick children? Kind of like Mother Theresa only more entertaining and funny. Like Whoopie Goldberg in "Sister Act." I would also continue my act in street theater, but would donate all proceeds from my purple felt hat to the convent. And I wouldn't expect Saint-hood or anything, I just want to do the things I love, and that's serving God and children and juggling (in that order).

So can I come and join you as a nun? If you didn't want me to leave the convent, I could do juggling webinars. I would really love that! Please tell me soon because I'm planning to sell all of my things so that I'm ready to move in.

Thank you so much, and blessings to you,
(Master Juggler and Future Nun) Elissa McKenzie

Apparently the Carmelite Sisters of the Divine
Heart of Jesus don't need a juggling nun…

Perhaps a slight edit is in order…

4

From: faith5239 [mailto:faith5239@gmail.com]

Sent: Thursday, March 17, 2011 7:17 PM

To: convent@suscopts.org

Subject: question about a calling

Dear St. Mary Convent,

I'm twenty-two and a life-long Catholic. I love the Lord more than anything in this entire world, and I live my life for serving Him. I have long considered a life dedicated to God as a nun, and I really think that's where I want my life to be. I've read your whole website about receiving the calling, and I understand. I also, however, have a serious love for helping children in need through Pediatrics. I'm an "A" student on track to enter medical school and become a Pediatrician. In order for me to fulfill both dreams of my life, is it possible to become a part-time nun? I promise I would keep all of my vows (such as no sex) even when I'm working at the hospital helping sick children, or at the dorm, where it's much harder! If this is not possible, then is there such a thing as a Dr. nun? In other words, could I become a doctor and also a nun? Perhaps in that way, I could live as a nun but also help sick children? Kind of like Mother Theresa only with credentials. And I wouldn't expect Saint-hood or anything, I just want to do the things I love, and that's serving God and children (in that order).

So can I come and join you as a nun? If you didn't want me to leave the convent, I could take classes online. I would really love that! Please tell me soon because I'm planning to sell all of my things so that I'm ready to move in.

Thank you so much, and blessings to you,

Sincerely,
(future Doctor) Elissa McKenzie

On Mon, Mar 21, 2011 at 11:49 PM, St. Mary
Convent <convent@suscopts.org> wrote:

Dear Ms. Faith:

Thank you for your email and your interest to
visit our convent. In regards to your concerns
about the life of celibacy and joining the
convent we have forwarded your email to His
Grace Bishop Xxxxxxx who is willing to discuss
the matter directly with you. Please contact
him at this email Xxxx@suscopts.org

May The Lord bless your life
St Mary Convent

From: faith5239 [mailto:faith5239@gmail.com]

Sent: Wednesday, March 23, 2011 2:38 PM

To: Xxxx@suscopts.org

Subject: Re: question about a calling

Dear Bishop Xxxxxxx,

In accordance with the letter from the Sister Mary Convent, please read my message below. I thank you most graciously in advance for taking your valuable time to consider my questions and provide much needed guidance.

Thank you again, and I eagerly await your reply.

Be blessed,
Elissa McKenzie

From: faith5239 <faith5239@gmail.com>

Subject: Re: question about a calling

Date: March 22, 2011 at 11:50:25 AM EDT

To: convent@suscopts.org

Dear Ms Sister-Madam-Lady-Holiness,

Thank you so much for passing this on, and responding so quickly. I would LOVE to speak with Bishop Xxxxxxx, but I am legally deaf and rely on email communication for just about everything. I use closed-captioning for watching tv, and our church has that on a big screen during service, so although I can't enjoy the music, I do hear the message.

Please, PLEASE ask Bishop Xxxxxxx if he would be willing to write to me with his thoughts on this -- I would be so grateful. I know he's very busy but I would truly value his wisdom on this question. So far no one at my church could offer much insight.

Thank you again very much, and blessings,
Elissa McKenzie

p.s. "Xxxxxxx" sounds Jewish - you guys are really modern!

On Thu, Mar 24, 2011 at 1:51 AM,
Bishop Xxxxxxx <xxxx@suscopts.org> wrote:
Peace and grace

I think we need to talk about it in person,
where do you live and how can we meet?

God bless you
Bishop Xxxxxxx
Coptic Orthodox Diocese of the Southern United
States

From: faith5239 [mailto:faith5239@gmail.com]

Sent: Saturday, March 26, 2011 10:11 AM

To: xxxx@suscopts.org

Subject: Re: question about a calling

Dear Bishop Xxxxxxx,

Thank you so much for your reply. I have to admit I'm a little bit intimidated talking to a Bishop, but I do so appreciate your helping me. I'm currently in school up north, at Boston University. I wrote St. Mary's because I was born and raised in Ft. Myers, and have always intended to return to Florida for my work. I researched Convents in Florida and found something special in St. Mary's.

I'm sure there's someone up here I can meet with to discuss things in a general kind of way; I just thought since I know St. Mary's is the place for me, I would contact them directly.

So is it possible to be both a pediatrician and a nun? If there's even the slightest possibility, I would like to know, and if there's not, I would also like to know, but then I would want to know why. I guess that's really the first thing that has to be addressed.

Thank you so much again for your response. If you can answer my questions, that would be so great (even though I'm still quite intimidated!)

Blessings,
Elissa McKenzie

On Sat, Mar 26, 2011 at 7:38 PM,
Bishop Youssef <xxxx@suscopts.org> wrote:

Dear Elissa

Peace and grace

You may contact Fr. Xxxxxxx in St. Mark Coptic Church in Boston, he will be a great help for you.

As for consecration, you can be fully consecrated sister, and in this case, your medical knowledge will be used within the services of the church for example we have a clinic on Orlando for the poor and the needy, FL in which you can serve.

Also you can be partially consecrated, in this case, you will work as pediatrician and you may serve in the church in other times. But you will not be dressed or ordained as consecrated sister.

I hope this answers your question.

God bless you
Bishop Xxxxxxx
Coptic Orthodox Diocese of the Southern United States

From: faith5239 <faith5239@gmail.com>

Subject: Re: question about a calling

Date: March 30, 2011 at 3:28:45 PM EDT

To: xxxx@suscopts.org

Dear Bishop Xxxxxxx,

Thank you so much for this valuable information. I had no idea that this could be done, but I had the desire, so I'm extremely pleased that there is a way to merge my gift for healing with my calling.

And thank you for the referral to Fr. Xxxxxxxxx. I will contact him to move to the next step when the time is right.

Best to you and be blessed,
Elissa McKenzie

5

Dear Grand Biloxi Hotel and Casino,

I'll be staying in your wonderful resort the week of April 23 to see the legendary and hilarious Uncle Kracker. Your hotel gets the best entertainment! I'll also be there to "celebrate" my divorce, so I really need this get-away!
My Uncle has stayed with you every year for the last 8 years, and he recommended you with the highest praise. He tells me that your staff is second to none in customer service, which I really appreciate. In anticipation of my stay, I have an important request.

I'm a STRICT Catholic (besides the divorce) who attends Confession daily. I NEVER miss a day. Because of this, I will be bringing my own Confessional to the hotel. Also, my Priest, Father Quigley Haster, will be staying with me. For this reason I'll need two Queen beds. My Confessional is roughly the size of a double-wide phone booth, and I won't need any additional assistance in bringing it up to my room; Father Haster and I have moved it many times before when I've travelled over the years. The Confessional will fit into any standard passenger elevator. It's free-standing, so will not cause any damage to the walls or other décor in the room. We only ask that you allow us to transport (with a small, non-commercial-grade dolly) the Confession booth through the lobby and up to our room (or if there's a side elevator, that's fine too!) Just let me know the most convenient route for you.

Thank you in advance for accommodating my needs as a guest in your hotel. I truly appreciate your understanding. Please get back to me as soon as possible so that I can fix my reservations and purchase my Uncle Kracker tickets. Father Haster thinks he's a riot!

Thanks again,
Jerry Upshaw

Subject: Re: [Incident: 110317-000182]
Response to your question on harrahs.com –
Dear Grand Biloxi Hotel and Casino,

Date: March 18, 2011 at 1:14:01 PM EDT

Answer   03/18/2011 10:07 AM

Good morning Mr. Upshaw,

I believe Grand Biloxi may have received your email in error.

I checked the tour dates for Uncle Kracker and found out he will be performing in New Orleans on April 23rd, and not locally; therefore, I am transferring your email to our sister property in New Orleans. Enjoy your stay with them.

Sincerely,
Xxxxxxx Xxxxxxxx
Customer Service
Grand Biloxi

Subject: Re: [Incident: 110317-000182]
Response to your question on harrahs.com –

From: Xxxxxxxx Xxxxxxxx
[mailto:xxxxxxxxx@harrahs.com]

Sent: Tuesday, March 28, 2011 10:22 AM

To: Jerry Upshaw

Subject: Jerry Upshaw Confessional in my room

Mr. Upshaw,

Thank you for choosing Harrah's New Orleans. Your email was by far the best email I have received since working for this property. The VIP Services department is located in the casino, so the person that could best answer this question would be a hotel manager. I will be getting in touch with Xxxx Xxxxxx some time this morning, but I will need contact information from you, in order for him to assist. I do not see why you would not be able to have your confessional, but I want to verify with him first.

We look forward to your stay.

Sincerely,
Xxxxxxxx Xxxxxxxx
VIP Services Supervisor
504-533-XXXX
xxxxxxxxx@harrahs.com

From: faith5239 [mailto:faith5239@gmail.com]

Sent: Tuesday, March 29, 2011 1:34 PM

To: Xxxxxxxx Xxxxxxxx

Subject: Jerry Upshaw Confessional in my room

Dear Ms. Xxxxxxxx,

Thank you SO MUCH for taking the time to accommodate me -- the service at Harrah's is really second to none, and I knew that! Is this a VIP request? I had no idea -- I'm not sure if I should feel super important or like a pain the rear? (Father Haster will like that, though -- he's a bit full of himself!)

Anyway you have no idea how relieved I will be to confirm this. As I mentioned in my previous letter, Fr. Haster and I have done this before, so we have it down to a science! Just let me know once you have confirmed with Mr. Xxxxxx so that I can solidify my reservations.

Thanks so much again -- Uncle Kracker, here we come!

Speak soon,
Jerry Upshaw

On Wed, Mar 30, 2011 at 2:13 PM, Xxxxxxxx
Xxxxxxxx xxxxxxxxx@harrahs.com> wrote:

Mr. Upshaw,

I spoke with the hotel manager, and he
informed me that our regular sized double
bed room would not have enough space for your
confessional. However, he did suggest, that
upon check in you request to be upgraded to
a suite. This will ensure that you have more
than enough space, and an extra bed for your
guest. Suite upgrades do require an up charge
of 150 per night.

Should you have any questions or concerns do
not hesitate to ask.

Sincerely,
Xxxxxxxx

Xxxxxxxx Xxxxxxxx
VIP Services Supervisor
Harrah's New Orleans Casino & Hotel
xxx Canal St.
New Orleans, LA 70130
OFFICE: 504.533.XXXX
FAX: 504.533.XXXX
RESERVATIONS: 1-800-HARRAHS
EMAIL: xxxxxxxxx@harrahs.com

From: faith5239 <faith5239@gmail.com>

Subject: Re: Jerry Upshaw Confessional in my room

Date: March 30, 2011 at 3:22:12 PM EDT

To: Xxxxxxxx Xxxxxxxx <xxxxxxxxx@harrahs.com>

Dear Xxxxxxxx,

That's an EXCELLENT idea -- I can't wait to tell Father Haster -- he'll really appreciate the extra space for his cowboy boot collection (he never wears anything else!)

Thank you SO MUCH for your help and the great service from everyone at your hotel -- you guys always go the extra mile to ensure that your guests are happy, and I'm a loyal customer forever!

Best regards and we'll see you (and Uncle Kracker!) very soon!

Jerry Upshaw

6

From: faith5239 <faith5239@gmail.com>

Subject: Can I bring Holy water on the plane?

Date: March 30, 2011 at 3:22:12 PM EDT

To: Customer Service < https://www.aa.com/contact/forms?topic=#/ >

Dear American Airlines Customer Service,

I'm a Priest and will be traveling on your airline in one month from Sandusky to San Jose for a conference. I will need to bring some Holy Water with me. I'm flexible as to the amount, but it certainly needs to be more than the 2.5 ounces of liquid that is currently allowed to be carried on board; there are a LOT of sinners in San Jose! I can check the Holy

Water. Does that help? It will be securely stored in several medium-sized containers and marked, "Holy Water." Is this okay? Please advise as to any procedures that I must be aware of prior to my travel.

Thank you very much,
Father Joseph McClain

7

From: faith5239 <faith5239@gmail.com>

Subject: An important visitor question

Date: March 17, 2011 at 3:17:09 PM EDT

To: xxxxxxxxxxx@kcgolddome.org

Dear Reverend Monsignor Xxxxxxx,

I'm from Ohio and will be visiting Kansas City in one week. I go to mass every Sunday, and would like to attend your beautiful Cathedral mass while I'm there. I will be bringing my fourteen year-old Salmon-breasted Cockatoo, Harvey, on my trip and would like to know if I may bring Harvey to Sunday service. Like me, Harvey is a long-time Catholic, so this would not be his first time to mass. For your planning, we'd like to come to the 9 o'clock service, as Harvey takes his nap every day around noon.

As you may know, Cockatoos are quite intelligent, having the IQ of the average toddler and capable of a range of complex emotions, even able to appreciate music and dance. I'd like to say on Harvey's behalf that he truly enjoys the musical portions of worship, and frequently bobs his head frantically up and down in his joy for the Holy Spirit. In addition, Harvey has had the occasion of "healing" fellow parishioners of various ailments by repeatedly pecking them on the forehead with his beak. I'm not entirely sure if every person who was pecked was permanently healed, but I do believe with all my heart that Harvey is always well-intended. I'd also like to add that he is quite insistent on accepting Communion wafers, and as such it would be important that he can participate in this most holy sacrament.

In the interest of complete disclosure I will admit that our Father Enwright as well as several parishioners were not initially pleased when Harvey had a few "accidents" in the donation basket, but since then I've fitted him with a tiny bucket that snaps snugly under his tail, and although he was not initially interested, Harvey now wears the tiny bucket willingly and no one has since complained.

Finally, one last fact you may not know is that Cockatoos are monogamous, further demonstrating that their lifestyle choices are consistent with the teachings of the Catholic church, making Harvey a perfectly acceptable guest in the Lord's house.

I sincerely hope that my letter has conveyed all the wonderful qualities of Harvey as I know him, and that you will see as I do, just how special and unobtrusive he is. We've attended mass together for the last twelve years, and I so look forward to the two of us in prayer together at The Cathedral for the Immaculate Conception.

Please confirm that this will be okay. We look forward to seeing you next Sunday.

Sincerely,
Olivia McClain (and Harvey)

From: <xxxxxxxxx@kcgolddome.org>

Subject: An important visitor question

Date: March 20, 2011 at 09:22:14 AM EDT

To: faith5239 <faith5239@gmail.com>

Dear Ms. McClain,

On behalf of Monsignor Xxxxxxx, I'm sorry to inform you that the only animals allowed in Mass are licensed service dogs. We hope this isn't too much of an inconvenience and we look forward to welcoming you this coming Sunday. Please tell Harvey it's nothing personal.

Have a blessed day,
Xxxxxx Xxxxxxx,
Executive Assistant to the Reverend Monsignor
Xxxxxx X. Xxxxxxx

8

From: faith5239 <faith5239@gmail.com>
Subject: Confession booth question
Date: March 17, 2011 at 3:19:02 PM EDT
To: webmaster@sacredheartfla.org

Dear Father Xxxxx,

I'm a master carpenter (like Jesus) of twenty-five years who's recently moved to Florida. I love to fish (also like Jesus!) I just bought a great house on a canal, three bedrooms, a doc out back, and a really nice lanai. I plan to live here for the rest of my life, and since my beloved wife died three years ago, I can decorate this place however I want. We were both Catholics our whole lives, and of course I still am (although I guess Frances is still Catholic in Heaven!). I can't get around like I used to because my hip is giving me problems (a rare carpentry-related affliction). So besides fishing from my pier, I'm mostly home, and that's fine with me; I love my new place. But the one thing that's missing is a place to give confession. I would really like to buy a confession booth. Can you assist me? If you have an extra one, can I buy it? If you don't, where can I buy one? I've looked online with no success. I really want to confess in a proper confessional – God would know the difference, and I don't want to be lazy about something so important. So please help me. Please tell me how much one of your confession booths would cost. I'll pay for transportation to Sebring, that's no problem at all. I know there are a lot of churches I could ask, but I don't know anyone here yet, and your church is so beautiful! From the first time I saw your website, I felt so welcome and loved, and I just knew that a confession booth from your church would have extra-special God blessings surrounding it! Please let me know as soon as possible how to purchase the booth from you, my confessions are really piling up!

I thank you in advance for your help and understanding with this challenging task.

Also, is it possible to confess by email? Is
that recognized in Heaven? Let me know.

Very sincerely,

Thomas Crowley, Jr.
Sebring, FL

From: faith5239 <faith5239@gmail.com>

Subject: SECOND EMAIL REQUEST - PLEASE RESPOND

Date: March 27, 2011 at 11:24:29 AM EDT

To: webmaster@sacredheartfla.org

Dear Father Xxxxx,

Can you please respond to my email below sent on March 17? I'm really interested in obtaining a Confessional booth. If you can't help me, perhaps you know of another church that would part with one? Please respond. I await your reply.

Thank you very much,
Thomas Crowley, Jr.

Still waiting to hear from Father Reitz...

9

Dear Islamic Society of Tampa Bay,

I'm a life-long resident of Tampa, and I just love it here. Over the years I've had a LOT of jobs, I've cleaned school buses, walked dogs, delivered Chinese food, trimmed parakeet feathers at a vet, and I even worked at an animal shelter cleaning out the cages – yuk! For the last year, I've really been lucky in my business. It took a lot of years of

40

dedication, but finally my dream has paid off and I can do what I love full-time. I shine shoes. It's a gift. That's why I'm writing to you. Can I shine your people's shoes while they pray? I would do a GREAT job! And I won't cause any problem. I could just leave a small box outside of the mosque for people to put tips, and by the time they come out, they have beautiful, shiny shoes, just like new! Everybody wins! Don't you guys pray a LOT? Like 5 times a day or something? That's A LOT OF SHOES! I figure with that kind of business I could really make a difference in the world with my gift for shoe-shining, especially in the summer rainy season!

Please let me know that this is okay. I plan to come next week on Wednesday and then you'll see the people will want me to come every day after that. I will bring my shoe-shine kit (of course), a medium-sized wooden box that I put the shoes on when I shine them, and a small cooler for myself with drinking water, a Subway sandwich and Skittles. I won't take up much room at all. Maybe 2 times a day I'll need to use the bathroom, but you have one, right?

So thank you for helping me fulfill my dream of shining shoes for people in need. Please let me know that next Wednesday is okay for me to start shining shoes for your people.

Thanks again. I can't wait to hear from you!

Best,
Earl Duggart

Guess not…

10

EMAILED 3/17/11

http://mybodynbalance.com/classes.htm
Contacted Xxxx via the website form:

Dear Xxxx,

I'm a health conscious Muslim woman who's lived in Dearborn for three months. Your fitness center is very impressive and state-of-the-art. I'm aware that you offer a variety of classes geared toward women's needs. While that is a good effort in addressing the conservative Muslim population of Dearborn, it's not enough. Can you please have a workout class for women in the burqa? I normally wear one in public, and it's uncomfortable for women like me to disrobe for exercise. I think a class like this would be very popular. In just one week I have fifteen friends who would greatly appreciate this service and would gladly pay extra. We request a class that has aerobics, stretching and some strength training. We like all of your classes, especially the, "Gams, Butts and Guts" class. We could do any of them.

Please consider adding this class to your schedule as soon as possible. My lady friends and I are ready to work out. Would it be too soon to come next week in the burqa? If you don't want to make a burqa-only class, we can just show up for our regular workout but there will be fifteen of us wearing the burqa from now on. Do you have any problem with this? Please confirm as soon as possible so that we do not have any interruption in our exercise. Thank you very kindly for accommodating our needs. We are truly grateful to you and look forward to our new, burqa workouts.

Kindest regards to your organization now and in the future,

H. Raffiah Nayalah

On Sat, Mar 19, 2011 at 6:04 PM, BODY N BALANCE (Xxxx Xxxx) <xxxxxxxxxxx@yahoo.com> wrote:

Hello~

I would like to meet with you in person, as I am not sure I got the correct idea from your email. You want to have 15 ladies join BNB, as long as we could have a "ladies only" class? You have seen the building I assume, as you spoke of it being "state of the art"...we have no blinds on the windows either. Wouldn't this be a problem as well? I do not work until 2pm on Monday, and will not be back on line until then...could you call or come in Monday between 2-5pm? There is however, a male instructor in at this time, but we can sit in my office. I look forward to speaking with you either in person (preferred) or via phone (313-792-XXXX) to see if we can make this work out for you ladies. Thank you for getting in touch with me...

Xxxx Xxxx
313.792.XXXX
www.mybodynbalance.com

Note:

- Every WED is sign up for following week
- Parking : the 2 spots under the awning only, or street.

From: faith5239 <faith5239@gmail.com>

Subject: Re: BODY N BALANCE

Date: March 19, 2011 at 6:21:21 PM EDT

To: "BODY N BALANCE (Xxxx Xxxx)"
<xxxxxxxxxxxx@yahoo.com>

Dear Xxxx,

Thank you so kindly for your prompt and kind response. Unexpectedly I have to be out of town next week, but I will instruct my sister, Bunevsha, to contact you for a time to meet. I'm uncertain of her schedule.

To summarize our request, our main priority is that we are able to work out with ladies (a ladies only class), and that we can wear the burqa, because as you say, there are windows and many other people about, but as long as we have on the burqa that is fine.

This is our hope. To exercise in the burqa for your "Gams, Butts and Guts" class in particular, but also for other classes. In this way, there would be no special arrangements necessary on your part, only that you allow us to exercise in the burqa.

Is there a dress code that prohibits this? Or can we come in the burqa?

If it is possible, please let me know. Otherwise, hopefully my sister can work to arrange this in my absence.

Thank you again very kindly for your dedication and assistance.

Sincerely,
H. Raffiah Nayalah

From: BODY N BALANCE (Xxxx Xxxx)
<xxxxxxxxxxxx@yahoo.com>

Date: Tue, Mar 22, 2011 at 3:39 PM

Subject: Re: Answers to your questions.

To: faith5239 <faith5239@gmail.com>

Thank YOU so much for the kind words! It means a lot to me when people compliment me, when I am just doing my job. I went into this field, trying to help people look and feel better, and a long the way...decided to be a gym owner that truly cared about it's members. All of my members are important to me...without them BODY N BALANCE would not be.

Have a great week & I look forward to hearing from you whenever it is convenient. ☺

Xxxx Xxxx
313.792.XXXX
www.mybodynbalance.com

Note:
- Every WED is sign up for following week
- Parking : the 2 spots under the awning only, or street.

CURRENT EVENT:"March Madness"
Refer 2 friends--get 1 month unlimited

On Tue, Mar 22, 2011 at 5:13 PM, BODY N
BALANCE (Xxxx Xxxx) <xxxxxxxxxxxx@yahoo.com>
wrote:

WEEK Mar 28-Apr 2..they fill FAST!

ALSO cardio circuit has been canceled for wed
Mar 23...but in it's place is TOTAL BODY *(not
plus)*... I have 5 spots open if you would like
it email me ASAP.

Xxxx Xxxx
313.792.XXXX
www.mybodynbalance.com

Note:
  - Every WED is sign up for following week
  - Parking : the 2 spots under the awning
    only, or street.

From: faith5239 <faith5239@gmail.com>

Subject: Re: TOMORROW (WED) is sign up
day... AND extra class.... tomorrow @ 6pm

To: "BODY N BALANCE (Xxxx Xxxx)"
<xxxxxxxxxxxx@yahoo.com>

Date: Wednesday, March 23, 2011, 3:28 PM

Thank you, Xxxx, for all of your valuable
assistance. I'm still out of town, but when
I hear from all of the ladies I will contact
you to be sure there's sufficient room in
the classes should we come all together. In
the meantime please don't reserve anything
special.

Best regards,
H. Raffiah Nayalah

From: "BODY N BALANCE \(Xxxx Xxxx\)" <xxxxxxxxxxxx@yahoo.com>

Subject: Re: TOMORROW (WED) is sign up day... AND extra class.... tomorrow @ 6pm

Date: March 23, 2011 at 3:35:19 PM EDT

To: faith5239 <faith5239@gmail.com>

Thank you ...and enjoy your trip!

Xxxx Xxxx
313.792.XXXX
www.mybodynbalance.com

Note:
- Every WED is sign up for following week
- Parking : the 2 spots under the awning only, or street.

CURRENT EVENT:"March Madness"
Refer 2 friends--get 1 month unlimited!

11

EMAILED 3/21/11

http://www.skydiveswflorida.com/contact.htm

info@skydiveswflorida.com

Dear SkyDive Southwest Florida,

I would like to schedule a tandem skydive jump with your company for me and four of my sisters. It would be our first ever. We're nuns, so we will have to wear the habit. Will this be a problem? The other Sisters and I couldn't decide if it would interfere with the jumping, or would act as a helpful break and thereby assist in the descent. In any case, it's important that we wear it. We would really like to do this in approximately 3 weeks, after Easter (that's a busy time for us). Please let me know.

Thank you kindly for your assistance,

Sister Mary K. H.
St. Catherine's Convent

p.s. Last year we ran in a half marathon in
the habit and it was just great!

On Tue, Mar 22, 2011 at 10:43 PM, Skydive Southwest Florida <info@skydiveswflorida.com> wrote:

Dear Sister Mary,

Thanks for your e-mail and your interest in skydiving. Your request is pretty unique so far. Before we answer, well need to know how your habit is exactly. Can you send us a picture.

Blue skies,
Xxxx Xxxxx
863-675-XXXX

Quoting faith5239 <faith5239@gmail.com>:

Dear Xxxx,

Did you receive my last email with the picture?
The Sisters and I eagerly await your response.
I sent it on March 23.

Thank you and God Bless,
Sister Mary K. H.

On Sun, Mar 27, 2011 at 5:53 PM,
Skydive Southwest Florida
<info@skydiveswflorida.com> wrote:

Dear Sister Mary,

Yes we did receive your previous e-mail. After reviewing it, hula hoops looks like a lot of fun.

Blue skies,
Xxxx Xxxxx

Quoting faith5239 <faith5239@gmail.com>:

Dear Xxxx,

I'm sorry, I'm a bit confused. I'm not writing about hula hoops, as I mentioned to you, I cannot send a picture of myself, and so downloaded a picture from the internet that although amusing, does at least convey what a nun's habit looks like. I'm sorry if that wasn't clear. Can you please let me know if my Sisters and I will be able to skydive while wearing our habits? That was my original question.

Thank you kindly,
Sister Mary

On Mon, Mar 28, 2011 at 12:02 PM,
Skydive Southwest Florida
<info@skydiveswflorida.com> wrote:

Dear Sister Mary,

After reviewing the picture with the instructors, we decided not to do it with the nun's habit for 2 reasons:

1) the habit is in the way to put the harness on safely
2) too much fabric flying around that could become a hazard during the freefall or in case of emergency

We always put safety first.

Let us know.

Blue skies,
Xxxx Xxxxx
863-675-XXXX

From: faith5239 <faith5239@gmail.com>
Subject: Re: Skydive inquiry
Date: March 28, 2011 at 4:29:12 PM EDT
To: Skydive Southwest Florida
<info@skydiveswflorida.com>

Dear Xxxx Xxxxx,

The Sisters will be so disappointed, as am I, however we completely respect the measures of safety that your highly professional team observe. I'm sure we can find another unique interest for our fundraiser that is closer to earth. That must be where God wants us to stay!

Thank you so much for your consideration and advice. We will pray for your continued safety and prosperity.

Be blessed,
Sister Mary K. H.

12

From: faith5239 <faith5239@gmail.com>

Subject: Question about a burial

Date: March 17, 2011 at 3:20:52 PM EDT

To: info@fortmyersmemorial.com

Dear Ft. Myers Memorial Gardens,

My late husband (God rest his soul) has been at peace in your cemetery for eleven years now. Years ago we bought a three-space family plot for me, my husband, and our daughter. Much to our surprise, our daughter has been married for some time now and she no longer wants to use the family plot because she wants to be buried next to her husband. For the last year, I was wondering what to do with the extra space, but yesterday God sent me the solution: Can I have my husband's pot-bellied pig, Earl, buried next to him? Earl died this week, and he was EVERYTHING to my husband, I think he loved that pig more than he loved me! Earl was large for a pot-belly, weighing 308 pounds, but I think he would still fit into a standard coffin, right?

In accordance with my husband's wishes, Earl needs to be buried in his blue-ribbon medal from the tri-county fair and his favorite purple blanket that my husband and Earl used to snuggle in together on chilly nights. His tombstone should read, "Here lies Earl: the best damn pig in the world." And he really was! My husband left money in his Will specifically for Earl's funeral, so the cost is not a problem. Even as great as Earl was, I personally don't want to be buried next to a pig, but this also is not a problem since Earl could be on one side of my husband, and I could eventually be on the other.

Please get back to me to confirm arrangements as soon as possible. Earl is currently on ice but Spring is coming and I can't wait very long. I live in Labelle, so I can bring Earl over as early as this week. Do we need an appointment or can we just show up? You have some kind of storage facility if we just show up, right? I would just need some help hoisting Earl out of the station wagon. I have help on this end but they can't come with me.

So thank you for helping Earl into his final resting place next to his favorite person in the whole world. I think Earl loved my husband more than I did! Please tell me the best day (very soon!) to bring Earl. If I don't hear back, then just plan on the end of this week, okay? That way you can at least take Earl, and we can talk about a day soon after to have the funeral.

Thank you so much, and God bless,
Cathleen Wheeler

From: info@fortmyersmemorial.com

Subject: Question about a burial

Date: March 18, 2011 at 9:12:38 AM EDT

To: faith5239 <faith5239@gmail.com>

Dear Mrs. Wheeler,

We are very sorry for your loss and blessed to have your husband resting in eternal peace with us here at Memorial Gardens. Unfortunately, we are not allowed by law to inter pets or any other animals not of the human variety on our grounds. We suggest you contact Earl's vet to have his remains interred in the proper place. And if it's any consolation, I think your impassioned request would make both your late husband (God rest his soul) and Earl, feel very honored.

Many Blessings,

Xxxxxx X Xxxxxx
Memorial Gardens Funeral Home Manager

From: faith5239 <faith5239@gmail.com>

Subject: Question about a burial

Date: March 17, 2011 at 3:20:52 PM EDT

To: info@fortmyersmemorial.com

Dear Mr. Xxxxxx,

I must admit I'm disappointed that Earl won't
be able to rest his 308 pounds eternally next
to my husband, they were quite the pair! But
I do understand and will call our vet asap,
Earl's starting to smell up the F-150 flatbed.

Thanks again and God bless!

Cate

13

From: faith5239 <faith5239@gmail.com>

Subject: Attention Rabbi Xxxx Xxxxxxx

Date: March 17, 2011 at 3:24:31 PM EDT

To: info@newschul.org

Dear Rabbi Xxxxxxx,

I'm writing on behalf of my nephew, who attends your temple and will be Bar Mitzvah soon.

You state in the, *New Shul Mitzvah Handbook* that "A creative interpretation of the Haftarah/ Torah portion (poetry, art, monologue, etc.) will be made by the student in lieu of a traditional Haftarah portion or "speech." Also he tells me that there's a new program emerging called, "Rap with the Rabbi." This gave my nephew a great idea and we're all very excited about it.

Can my nephew rap the torah for Bar Mitzvah? Believe me when I say that he's put a great deal of thought into this. For example the total number of rappers would be ten, symbolizing a Minyan. He would use words or phrases from the Talmud in the rap songs, and the names of the rappers are derived from the Pentateuch and other books of the Bible: Leviticus Brown, Jazzy G-Genesis, Deuteronomy Daddy-O, E-Z Exodus Fly, and Baby Face UnoDosTres (representing the Book of Numbers).

I think it's fairly straightforward, but to be clear, my nephew proposes to rap the Haftarah, particularly the traditional chant, at which point the rap would become a musical explosion of.Hebrew rhyme. I might add that Jazzy G-Genesis is an exceptional beat-boxer, so this portion of the rap would be especially exciting. (Our only question is, would the rappers themselves also need to be Jewish, or would it be acceptable if they just wear the Yarmulke?)

You should know that each of the Ten Commandments will be incorporated into the rap. For example, "Da-da-don't-mess-around-wit-da-

Word-above, don't-steal-or-fight, be-peace-n-luv-ya'll!"

My nephew is taking the teachings at the B'nai Mitzvah Academy very seriously, and wishes to merge his youthful spirit with the strength of rap as symbolism of the merging of boy and man.

Please let us know as soon as possible so my nephew can get the costumes fitted for the rappers (Jazzy G-Genesis is quite large and needs several fittings).

We eagerly await your thoughts,

B'shalom,
Dorit Mendel

On Fri, Mar 18, 2011 at 1:44 PM, Xxxx Xxxxx
<xxxxxx@templeisrael.net> wrote:

> Dear Dorit,
>
> Please let me know who your nephew is.
>
> Thank you,
> Rabbi Xxxx Xxxxx

-----Original Message-----

From: faith5239 [mailto:faith5239@gmail.com]

Sent: Fri 18/03/2011 13:52

To: Xxxx Xxxxx

Subject: Re: Important Bar Mitzvah question

He asked me not to say unless this was okay.
I don't want to embarrass him,
nor go back on my word. So is this something
that can be considered?

Thank you,
Dorit

On Fri, Mar 18, 2011 at 2:07 PM,
Jody Cohen <xxxxxx@templeisrael.net> wrote:

Dorit,

When a family has a question about a life
cycle event at the temple, we ask them to
please speak directly with the rabbi.

Thank you,
Rabbi Xxxx Xxxxx

From: faith5239 <faith5239@gmail.com>

Subject: Re: Important Bar Mitzpha question

Date: March 18, 2011 at 2:12:03 PM EDT

To: Xxxx Xxxxx <xxxxxx@templeisrael.net>

Thanks very much for your assistance. I'll tell my nephew.

Blessings,
Dorit

14

From: faith5239 <faith5239@gmail.com>
Subject: group of guest coming to your gym
Date: April 27, 2011 at 11:14:09 AM EDT
To: xxxx@mygoldsgym.com

Dear Gold's Gym,

I'm a personal assistant writing on behalf of Sheik Abdullah Amazid del Hamid of Qatar, High Council to the Consortium of Physicians Education Group of The Middle East. Sheik and his twelve colleagues will be attending a conference in Ft. Myers in late May, and would like to attend your gym for fitness during their one-week stay. You gym comes highly recommended and we are told that your facilities are the best in the city.

The Sheik is prepared to purchase either a temporary membership for the group, or even an annual if necessary. If our group is going to utilize your fine facilities, there are certain preparations that must be made in advance of our arrival.

The Sheik and group are, of course, Muslim, and as such practice prayer five times a day. Should their workout coincide with one of these prayer times, they will cease exercise and lay out their prayer mats for such a purpose. Nothing will be required of you, we only ask that prayer be allowed to commence with no interruption for the 10 minutes or so that it takes. Also, if someone in your gym knows how to chant the "Call to Prayer," that would be great. Otherwise let me know and we will bring our own Chanter.

Second, Muslims are a very clean people who practice daily ablutions and who use water in the cleansing after bathroom activities. As such, bathrooms in The Middle East are equipped with shower-heads by the toilets. Obviously you have no such equipment, so we request that you install Water-pics (the tooth-cleaning product) in each toilet stall that our men can use in place of the shower head (We're not requiring Water-picks specifically; I only thought of this due to the portability of them and also the speed of the jets is rather nice). If you have a different idea than the water-pics, that's fine.

I think that is all that we require. The Shiek is a very generous man and will show his gratitude for your hospitality I'm sure. Please confirm that you will be able to accommodate us with regards to prayer and water picks (or other option).

Thank you very kindly for your service in these matters. We look

forward to taking exercise in your gym.

p.s. I neglected one very important thing: are there women working in the same area of the gym? If so, we would need to rent the facility specifically for men during the workouts. Money is no object for this. Thank you. I wait your reply

Still waiting to hear from Gold's Gym...

15

From: faith5239 <faith5239@gmail.com>

Subject: Important visitor question for next week

Date: March 17, 2011 at 3:26:11 PM EDT

To: xxxxx@beachbaptist.org

Dear Rev. Xxxxxxx,

My sister attends your church (I live in Sarasota) and she just loves it! You're definitely touched by the Spirit in your sermons, which are so uplifting! I've attended twice and felt so rejuvenated afterwards. Both my sister and I were raised Baptist, and her children are of course raised the same. I live alone, except for my yellow lab, Sweeny.

Sweeny's two, and second to the Lord, he's just the greatest joy of my life!

That's why I'm writing to you. I visit my sister often, and the next time I'm down, I'd like to have Sweeny Baptized. He's the perfect dog, and I can't bear to think of him not going to Heaven. I don't know how many animals are there, or if they have a special animal Heaven, but whatever good place that dead dogs go is certainly where Sweeny will belong, and I would hate for him to get rejected on a technicality.

Can you please help us? I promise that Sweeny is a GREAT dog, and would be perfectly behaved for the whole ceremony (no peeing in the Holy water!). He loves to swim, so being dunked would be no problem.

Please let me know. Sweeny and I are coming down in a week, and I'll bring him to services in case you can do it then. Otherwise, we can schedule it when we see you.

Thanks so much! And by the way, I like your slogan, "Soaking up the *son*" very clever!

Speak soon and God bless,

Sincerely,
Ana Court and Sweeny

On Mar 27, 2011, at 11:29 AM, faith5239
wrote:

Dear Rev. Xxxxxxx,

I know you're very busy with sermons and prayer
requests and lots of other Godly things, but
can you please respond to my email from March
17 below? Sweeny and I are just as needy as
everyone else with our request, and I would
really like your help. Please let me know if
you can help us. I plan my trip around it, and
am waiting.

Thank you so much,
Ana Court

On Mon, Mar 28, 2011 at 10:28 PM, Xxxxx
Xxxxxxx <xxxxx@beachbaptist.org> wrote:

Hey Ana -

Sorry it took me so long to get back to you.
I'm actually at a loss with your request. I
want to be as sensitive as possible, but I
also do not wish to give you any sense of a
false hope.

I simply cannot find any scriptural backing
for animals going to heaven. The issue would
be the lack of a soul. The soul is actually
where the decisions for Christ must be made -
not in the physical body.

Taking Sweeny thru the baptism waters will
not do anything - just like it doesn't do
anything for a human except paint a picture
on the outside of what happens when a person
accepts Christ as Saviour on the inside.

Please don't think I don't care, but I can't
lie to you. Baptizing Sweeny and telling you
he will go to heaven would be doing just that.

I would love to counsel you further on this
issue if you would like and do hope you will

introduce yourself the next time you are in town.

In HIS service,
Xxxxx

From: faith5239 <faith5239@gmail.com>

Subject: Re: Second email from a guest please respond

Date: March 29, 2011 at 2:43:58 PM EDT

To: Xxxxx Xxxxxxx <xxxxx@beachbaptist.org>

Dear Pastor Xxxxxxx,

Thanks so much for getting back to me with such a kind and thoughtful way of breaking this terrible news to me. I don't like it, but if you say Sweeny isn't going to Heaven then I'm not in a position to argue. It's not the first time I've heard that, but then there was this kid on CNN who had a near-death experience and said that Heaven was very colorful and had dogs in it. He even wrote a book with his parents, and his dad is a Pastor of some church (can't remember where). Anyway I was glad to hear it, because as I said, Sweeny is the best dog ever!

My sister will have a good laugh at my expense but I'm still not going to tell Sweeny. I guess this means there's no hope for my Silver-breasted Cockatoo, Duke.

Thanks again for your guidance on this, I truly appreciate it. And I still like your slogan, "Soaking up the Son" -- genius!

God bless,
Ana and (still the greatest) Sweeny

16

From: faith5239 <faith5239@gmail.com>
Subject: Bar Mitzvah question
Date: March 17, 2011 at 4:36:11 PM EDT
To: hbtoffice@templehbt.org

Dear Temple Hillel B'nai Torah,

I live in the Back Bay, and I found your Temple online. You seem to be very inclusive; open to people from all backgrounds and situations. I live alone except for my two cats, Mitsy and Mr. Peterson, and my dog, Blakely. I'm writing because I would like to get my dog Blakely Bar Mitzvah. He's a boy (obviously), and is almost two, the time in dog years that would symbolize that puppy-into-dog period of life. I live a strictly Kosher life, and except for a few Saturday exceptions, I take my faith very seriously. As such, I would sleep better knowing that my home and all of those in it are indeed respecting my faith. I'm not going to have Mitsy Bat Mitzvah or Mr. Peterson Bar Mitzvah, because although they're affectionate animals, they don't want to keep Kosher and Mr. Peterson refuses to wear a Yarmulke (I'm thinking of sending them to my niece's in Boca, to be honest). Regarding Blakely, however, this is really a priority. Can you host a Bar Mitzvah for him? Of course I would provide a generous donation to your Temple, particularly since Blakely can't actually read the Torah portions that would normally be recited! He can bark a little bit of "Fiddler on the Roof," but that's hardly adequate! If you can help me, I would be forever grateful. It would be a small affair, really only Blakely, myself, my niece, and possibly Mitsy and Mr. Peterson if they're behaving, otherwise just the three of us and Blakely's vet, who's been a wonderful support for Blakely's spiritual journey.

Thank you very much for helping me in this most important matter. Please advise how to proceed. I look forward to hearing from you very soon. I need to do this before Blakely's second birthday, in three months!

Thank you again,

Most sincerely,
Elizabeth Solomon

17

From: faith5239 <faith5239@gmail.com>

Subject: Request for your services

Date: March 17, 2011 at 4:38:49 PM EDT

To: xxxxxxxxxxx@comcast.net

Dear Rabbi Xxxxxx,

I'm a life-long, practicing Jew who takes my faith very seriously. I keep Kosher and observe all holidays and customs. I married a wonderful Jewish woman and together we have been blessed with five children! We are in complete harmony with our lives, except for one thing. Can you circumcise our dog? We adopted him a year ago and love him very much, but his gentile manhood is a glaring problem in our perfect Jewish home! He's already neutered, but that doesn't address this problem. Last week my 5 year-old son asked why Noah (the dog) has such a funny wiener and why he doesn't have to have it snipped. I didn't have a good answer because of course all of the males in our home must have this! Like the rest of us, Noah also keeps Kosher and observes all other Jewish traditions (He will even wear a Yarmulke if I put it on him!)

So can you help us? I really need to address this issue in our family, particularly with young, impressionable children around. I believe everyone in our household serves as an example to Holy Jewish customs, and Noah is no exception, especially when we're all forced to see his private parts every day!

Please let me know the soonest time that I can schedule a Briss. I would like the same ceremony that would be afforded anyone else, including undergoing the *Mikveh* if possible; the last thing I want is for Noah to be discriminated against just because he's a dog. He's still part of the family, and as much as he can be, a Jew.

Thank you so much for your help and under-standing. I promised my son I would correct this, and I look forward to hearing from you soon.

Best regards and blessings,
Saul Weitzman

Sat, Apr 23, 2011 at 2:22 PM, Shelly Crouch <xxxxxx.xxxxxx@vcahospitals.com <mailto:xxxxxx.@vcahospitals.com>> wrote:

Dear Mr. Weitzman,

I am a little confused with your request . Dogs do not have the extra skin that covers their penis. They have a bone in their penis that must be covered by their prepuce to prevent health issues. Are you asking for a penis amputation? If that is the case we do not do this procedure unless health issues are involved. I am sorry we cannot help you in this matter if you have any other questions please feel free to give us a call.

Thank you , Xxxxxx Xxxxxx

VCA Miracle Mile Animal Clinic
XXXX Cleveland Ave.
Fort Myers, Fl 33901
239-936-XXXX<tel:239-936-XXXX>

From: faith5239 [faith5239@gmail.com]

Sent: Saturday, April 23, 2011 11:54 AM

To: Xxxxxx Xxxxxx
<xxxxxx.xxxxxx@vcahospitals.com
<mailto:xxxxxx.@vcahospitals.com>

Subject: Re: Noah

Dear Ms. Xxxxxx,

Oh my goodness, no! I had NO IDEA that dogs had a bone in their penis, that's quite remarkable! I would certainly NEVER suggest to cause harm to our beloved family pet; thank you so much for enlightening me about this.

I wonder if there might be a more appropriate pet for our Orthodox Jewish family. Are there any pets that CAN be circumsized?

Thank you again,
Saul W.

On Sat, Apr 23, 2011 at 3:26 PM, Shelly
Crouch <Xxxxxx.Xxxxxx@vcahospitals.com>
wrote:

I dont know of any that can be but you might
consider finding a female pet to adopt. Good
luck in your search.

Thank you , Xxxxxx Xxxxxx

VCA Miracle Mile Animal Clinic
XXXX Cleveland Ave.
Fort Myers, Fl 33901
239-936-XXXX

From: faith5239 <faith5239@gmail.com>

Subject: Re: Noah

Date: April 23, 2011 at 3:32:09 PM EDT

To: Xxxxxx Xxxxxx
<Xxxxxx.Xxxxxx@vcahospitals.com>

Wow -- talk about stating the obvious -- a female pet -- of course! (My wife says that sometimes I over-complicate things -- I guess she's right!)

Thank you again very much, and be blessed!

Saul

18

EMAILED VIA THEIR FORM ON 3/27/11

http://www.saintjohntheevangelist.com/
contact-us

Sent to Saint John the Evangelist Church in
Naples

Dear Father Xxxx,

I attend Mass regularly and receive the Holy
sacrament. I've done so since I was a child,
and every week of my life I think the same
thing: the Communion wafers taste terrible.
Is there any possibility to flavor them? You
could have lots of variety, such as berry,
cheddar cheese, and tropical fruit. I just
came up with those but there are lots of
possibilities.

In addition to being a good Catholic, I'm also quite a good cook, so perhaps I could help to modify the wafers for you. Please let me know if this is something you would consider. After hundreds of years of the same model, maybe it's time for a change.

Thank you most respectfully for considering this improvement to our Communion wafers.

God bless,
Myrna Burke

From: XXXXXXXX <http://www.
saintjohntheevangelist.com/contact-us>

Subject: Question about Communion wafers

Date: March 30, 2011 at 1:14:02 PM EDT

To: faith5239 <faith5239@gmail.com>

Dear Ms. Burke,

Your observation of Communion wafers is certainly understandable and gave our Ladies' Prayer Group quite a chuckle! Unfortunately we're unable to administer the many details of inventing new wafer flavors, having no test kitchen, complying to FDA regulations, etc. Maybe we could move up to graham crackers or something, you've got us thinking!

Be Blessed,
Father Xxxx

19

EMAILED 3/17/11 to website contact form:

Subject: Can you make a Confession booth for me?

http://www.infinityexhibits.com/pages/Contact.html

Infinity Exhibits

XXXX Holland Dr., Ste X

Boca Raton, Fl. 33487

Dear Infinity Exhibits,

I've studied your website and there's no doubt that you can create just about anything. I also noticed that you have a, "custom design" tab, which is why I'm writing to solicit your services. Although I was raised Hindu, in my adulthood I've become a strict Catholic. It's just the religion for me. In my growth as a Catholic over the last fifteen years, I've found that I need more time with God than just that spent going to Mass.

For this reason, I would like to have a Confession booth in my home. A confession booth is about the same size as a double-wide phone booth. I'm not particular about the material, but I would prefer if it can be painted in a deep Burgundy color, symbolizing the blood of Christ. Also the inside would need to have a comfy cushion-type bench in each side (obviously), preferably with a satin-finish padded cloth seat, also in burgundy. On the outside centered over the two doors, I'd like a hand-carved looking placard that reads, "Jake's Confession Booth" in any font style, as long as it's religious looking.

Please let me know how long it will take you to make my Confession booth, the cost, and estimated time of completion. The good news is that I live in Ft. Myers, so I could drive directly to your offices in Boca and pick it up - no shipping!

Thanks very much for your fine craftsmanship and service. I look forward to hearing from you soon—I'm very excited and already saving up things to confess!

Thanks again, and God bless,
Rajiv Chattopadhyay

Still waiting to hear from Infinity Exhibits…

20

Campbell's Soup Ideas for Innovation product idea submission

http://www.campbellsoupcompany.com/ideas/submitidea.aspx

Subject: Last-Supper Soup!

Message:

Christians are a huge market in the United States, and it would be just GREAT to have a vegetable soup called, Last Supper Soup, with pasta in the shapes of the apostles! You could also have shapes of other Biblical characters, such as Noah's ark, Adam and Eve, a cross or crucifix, and so on, and even Jewish characters like a menorah, Jewish star, Moses, etc. So what do you think? It would

be great! And you could pair The Last Supper
Soup with your Goldfish crackers, which are a
symbol of Christ! Fantastic!

From: Kristy Welch

Thank you!

Your idea has been submitted!

We sincerely appreciate your interest in Campbell Soup Company. We will contact you after the appropriate Campbell representatives have reviewed your submission. Please allow up to 3-6 months for us to reply to your submission.

Your confirmation number is 03-21-2011-15-16-09-6722. You may print this page for your records.

Terms and Conditions

You accepted Campbell's Terms and Conditions for submitting your idea.

Your Contact Information

Miss Kristy Welch
12199 Lucca St. #202
Ft. Myers, FL 33966
239-565-4672
faith5239@gmail.com

Your Idea

Category: New Products - Soups
Title: Last Supper Soup

Your Idea: Christians are a huge market in the United States, and it would be just GREAT to have a vegetable soup called, Last Supper Soup, with pasta in the shapes of the apostles! You could also have shapes of other Biblical characters, such as Noah's ark, Adam and Eve, a cross or crusifix, and so on, and even Jewish characters like a minorah, Jewish star, Moses, etc. So what do you think? It would be great! And you could pair The Last Supper Soup with your Goldfish crackers, which are a symbol of Christ! Fantastic!

Intellectual Property Information

You did not register this idea.

You do not share ownership rights in this idea.

Current Development Status: **It's just a fantastic, God-inspired idea to give to the world!**

You have not submitted this idea to any person, company or other entity.

21

http://www.newshowstudios.com/submit/

EMAILED 4/27/11 VIA THEIR WEBSITE FORM

PITCHING MY TV SHOW IDEA, MUSLIMS AFTER DARK!

MESSAGE: In response to the growing Muslim population and the greater need for Muslim programming, and because in America sex sells, I propose the late-night 30-minute show called, "Muslims After Dark!" This will be a flashy, quick-editing, series of videos that show women in Burqa's flashing various body parts, such as a wrist, an ankle, an wow, look out – a knee! Muslim guys with elbow fetishes will go crazy! Saucy music will play as Burqa-clad women sway their hips and teasingly pull their Burqa to reveal the naughty body part! Muslims After Dark is a high-concept, low-production cost idea that will leave

Muslim guys biting their fingernails off in frustration! Once the show is a hit, can't you just see the Muslims After Dark! Calendar, coffee mugs, and t-shirts? Then we can go with a live webcam and subscribers, there's no limit to the money this can make! I can't wait to hear your thoughts about this golden idea! Thanks very much, your site is the best thing ever for bringing quality programming to our airwaves!

Still waiting to hear from New Show Studios...

22

From: faith5239 <faith5239@gmail.com>

Subject: Important new product question

Date: March 17, 2011 at 4:55:19 PM EDT

To: customerservice@syfobeverages.com

Dear Syfo Beverages,

I'm from Port Charlotte, Florida and have been a loyal customer of Syfo ever since I tried your lemon-lime Syfo at a party three years ago. Your delicious water is the ultimate in high quality standards in every area: I've done a LOT of market research, and you guys have the cleanest, purest water around!

Because you have such a high standard (and because I love your product and your company outlook so much) I'd like to propose a new product to you that's really lacking in the market place. While studying your website, I noticed that your water is "Kosher." That's great for the Jewish market, and hey, those are God's chosen people, so…..can't forget them, right!

But still, I think you're missing a HUGE market: the Christians! I think you should include bottled Holy water in your product line – this would be TREMENDOUS! As a lifelong Christian and supporter of Holy water, I've found that it not only cleanses my soul, but it also cleanses my body. You should sell this RIGHT AWAY. You could still have Holy Tangerine, Holy Cherry, and my favorite, Holy Lemon-lime. I'm sure you didn't mean to, but seriously, you've been so focused on the Jewish market that you've somewhat forgotten the Holy-roller Christians, you know?

Please develop this much needed drink. We Christians would LOVE it, and only a fantastic company like Syfo could do Jesus justice! If you need any consulting advice, just let me know. I'm happy to assist (free of charge!).

By the way, I thought Kosher food had to be blessed by a Rabbi. Do you use a staff Rabbi, or is it by district, or what?

Thanks so much for your fantastic water, I'm
a loyal customer!

Best regards,

Jeremy McClain
Port Charlotte, Florida

On Mon, Mar 21, 2011 at 5:41 PM,
Syfo Beverages Customer Service
<customerservice@universalbeverages.com>
wrote:

Dear Mr. McClain,

Thank you for complimenting our company on the purity of our water. We really appreciate it when a customer understands how much emphasis we place on water purity and the intensive steps we take to thoroughly purify our water.

Your knowledge of our Syfo website implies that you have thoroughly reviewed our entire site, which is extremely gratifying to us. As you know, the Syfo story goes back to 1949 in New York City, when Charles Schussler sold syphons of seltzer water. Not long after, he relocated to Miami and Syfo beverages could be found in every Publix Super Market. This history gives Syfo products brand equity of over 50 years. Many early customers were no doubt Jewish seltzer drinkers and they are some of our longest loyal customers. However, we don't want to give the impression that our focus is on one religious group over another. At Syfo our focus is on the health conscious consumer and we hope our website reflects that about our products. Based on your email, we obviously could do a better job.

Many of our customers write to us with testimonials about how Syfo has helped them with their battles with obesity, high blood pressure, diabetes, gluten intolerance and food allergies. Kosher has come to be equated with strict food safety, cleanliness, and is universally considered to be all-natural and almost organic. Kosher products do well throughout the world. In fact Kosher products are a $150 billion market growing by 15% annually, a testament to its secular popularity.

To answer your question regarding how food is labeled Kosher, rabbis do not bless food to make it kosher. There are blessings that observant Jews recite over food before eating, but these blessings have nothing to do with making food kosher. Food can become kosher without a rabbi ever becoming involved with it. Vegetables from you garden for instance are kosher (as long as they don't have any bugs, which are not kosher).
In order to certify a manufactured or processed product as Kosher, the manufacturing plant and all ingredients are subjected to an annual inspection by a local Rabbi who certifies that

the plant and materials meet the requirements of the Orthodox Union.

We are delighted that you as a long-time customer have such high regard for our products that you want us to market Syfo as Holy Water. (Long ago we thought of a great tag line…Syfo water is so pure, it is almost Holy). However, please consider that the success rate of bringing a new product to market is less than 1%. We really do value your opinion and have thought long and hard about the issues you brought up in your email. You will find if you continue to use our website that we try our best to respect and appropriately acknowledge all of our customers who celebrate Hanukah, Christmas, Passover or Easter during the year.

To thank you for your thoughtful email and for your customer loyalty to our products, we would like to send you a Publix gift card, which you can use to purchase your favorite Syfo products. Just email us with your address and we'll put one in the mail to you.

Xxxxx Xxxxxxx
Universal Beverages, Inc.
PO Box XXX
Ponte Vedra Beach, FL 32004
904-280-XXXX ~ 904-280-XXXX Fax
www.syfobeverages.com

From: faith5239 <faith5239@gmail.com>

Subject: Re: Reply to 3/17/11 email

Date: March 22, 2011 at 1:54:00 PM EDT

To: Syfo Beverages Customer Service
<customerservice@universalbeverages.com>

Dear Syfo Beverages,

WOW -- you guys are even more fantastic than I thought before -- thanks for your reply and all of that interesting information! I never knew about the annual Rabbi visit or that bugs aren't Kosher, but then I guess that's good news!

It's a bummer that new product launches only have a 1% success rate; I think the Holy Water idea is a great one! But hey, that tag line about Syfo being so pure it's almost Holy is GENIUS! You should use that!

And thanks for offering to send the gift card -- what a bonus!! I think in honor I'm going use it to have a Syfo party and tell everyone about all the Jewish-Kosher stuff I learned!

So thanks again, Syfo, your products are terrific and so are your people, I'm now an unshakable loyal customer!

Did you ever think of putting a picture of the Rabbi-Inspector guy on your bottles? That would be so cool!

Thanks again,
Jeremy (loyal customer) McClain

p.s. Almost forgot! Please send the gift card to me at:

XXXXXX Lucca St. #XXX
Ft. Myers, FL 33966!

And they did send me a bunch of coupons, go Syfo!

23

EMAILED ON 3/21/11

Dear Pepperidge Farms,

Your Goldfish line of snacks is ABSOLUTELY WONDERFUL, every flavor! My son is 4 and he really loves the pizza flavor and my daughter loves the colored ones, we buy tons of them!

I'm writing though because I'm Catholic and our church uses your Goldfish for Holy Communion (the original, cheddar flavor). My neighbor is Baptist and they also use the Goldfish for Communion on special occasions (also cheddar!). I've been asking around, and you have no idea how many people use your cheddar Goldfish for Communion! This is a huge market for you! So I thought it would be a great idea to bring out a new variety of Goldfish: they should still be cheddar, but just call them, "Body of Christ" Goldfish. What do you think? The Christian market would eat it up! (No pun intended).

There's no charge for this idea; it's a free gift for being such a great company! I just hope that one day I see the Body of Christ Goldfish snacks; that would be payment enough for me!

Sincerely your loyal Christian customer,
Kristy Welch

Still haven't heard back; Pepperidge Farms is great but they're no Syfo…

24

From: faith5239 <faith5239@gmail.com>

Subject: Important customer service question

Date: March 17, 2011 at 4:48:20 PM EDT

To: Xxxxxx.Xxxx@suntrust.com

Dear Ms. Xxxx,

I'm relocating to Miami and searching for a home bank for all of my banking and investment needs. As a strict Orthodox Jew, my faith prohibits members of the opposite sex to have physical contact. In the Orthodox religion, co-mingling or even having discourse are kept to an absolute minimum (I speak to my wife as little as possible, which is a great thing in our religion, so you can imagine that discussions between opposite sex strangers is absolutely inappropriate).

According to recent statistics, Miami has the largest Jewish population of any city except for New York. And many of us are Orthodox. Therefore, I think it's a good idea for your bank to provide separate banking centers for men and women. I realize this is a long-term project; on the other hand, you have several branches in Miami; why don't you simply divide them to have half of the branches for men and half for women? And of course, Gentiles wouldn't be prohibited from banking at these branches, so there would be no inconvenience (so long as the Gentiles respect the gender rules at each branch).

While you're in the process of this change, in the immediate future, could you please provide separate lines at my branch, at 777 Brickell Ave? That would really be wonderful.

Please let me know when the separate lines will begin so I can return to the bank (I get paid bi-weekly, so please let me know as soon as possible).

Thank you very much for your continued excellent customer service.

Most sincerely,
Eli Weinstein

From: Xxxx Xxxxxxxxxx
<x.xxxxxxxxxx@floridagulfbank.com>

Subject: FW: Contact Inquiry

Date: April 5, 2011 at 10:34:09 AM EDT

To: "faith5239@gmail.com"
<faith5239@gmail.com>

Dear Mr. Weinstein,

First let me thank you for your interest in Florida Gulf Bank. We are always honored when someone thinks enough of our bank and our employees to consider entrusting us to watch over and help with their finances. I apologize for taking so long to get back to you. I wanted to discuss your request with the Daniels office as well as the bank President, Mr. Xxxx Xxxxxxx.

Unfortunately we will not be able to accommodate your request for separate teller lines. I do however have a few options that hopefully you will find acceptable. As you are probably aware we do have a male employee at the Daniels office that is more than capable and could be made available to take care of the opening of your new account. We could make an appointment with him to ensure that he would be available when it is convenient for you. To take care of your day to day transactions I can offer you use of the drive thru, the atm machine and online banking. These alternative banking methods should limit any contact that you would have to have with a female employee of the bank.

Should you wish to precede with the opening of your account please feel free to email me or telephone Mr. Xxx Xxx at the Daniels office. His telephone number is 239-985-XXXX. Again thank you for your interest in Florida Gulf Bank, we look forward to having you as a client.

Xxxx Xxxxxxxxxx
Florida Gulf Bank
"The Power of Personal Service"
Client Relations Manager, VP
2247 First Street
Fort Myers, FL 33901
Phone 239-332-XXXX
Fax 239-226-XXXX

25

From: faith5239 <faith5239@gmail.com>

Subject: Portrait commission request

Date: April 23, 2011 at 2:00:55 PM EDT

To: xxxxxxx@ec.rr.com

Dear Mr. Xxxxxx,

I live in Florence, S.C. and have just gone through a vicious divorce with my wife of 12 years. I'm a strict Catholic and don't believe in divorce, but oh, how times have changed! She really showed her true colors and is convinced that I should pay her a LUDICROUS sum of alimony (we don't even have kids!). In any case, the attorneys are getting everything on both sides, so in an effort to end the madness, I've agreed to pay her what she wants (ouch!) under one condition to which she has reluctantly consented. As my part of the settlement, I will be painted as King Henry VIII, in full Kingly regalia with robe, scepter, fancy English outfit and crown – the only difference being my face instead of King Henry's, and not so fat of course. Also in the portrait, my wife will be kneeling at my left side, kissing my ring as I look regally out from the canvas, as a show of her gratitude for my magnanimous monthly support and as a reminder that in the days of King Henry she would have been getting the axe! Of course I would like the background to be filled out with Kingly accoutrements, such as a globe indicating that I am the master of all that I survey, a desk to illustrate my hard work and a fat wallet resting on top to illustrate my wealth. Also I would like my dog sitting contentedly on my right, showing what true loyalty is.

These items are just ideas that we could play around with. The point is to capture the essence of the new relationship between my soon-to-be ex-wife and myself: one of a tolerant man and his parasitic succubus. Also this should be quite large, as it will be prominently displayed over my fireplace mantle, by which I will parade countless guests to behold in its majestic and victorious splendor. Please contact me with the soonest dates that we can discuss and any deposits, photos and the like that you require.

Thank you very kindly for your fabulous work and your time. I look forward to hearing from you soon.

Best regards,
James P. Stridemore III

p.s. Your portrait of the ballerina at the piano is grace personified - you're truly gifted!

From: faith5239 <faith5239@gmail.com>

Subject: SECOND Portrait commission request

Date: May 10, 2011 at 3:15:09 PM EDT

To: xxxxxxx@ec.rr.com

Dear Mr. Xxxxx,

Are you in receipt of my email dated April 23? I'm very much interested in commissioning your services and realize that you may be booked for quite some time. Can you please read my portrait needs and let me know an approximate date for a sitting, or whether you can do this entirely from photographs?

Thank you very much,
James S.

From: Xxxxxxx <xxxxxxx@ec.rr.com>

Subject: Re: SECOND Portrait commission request

Date: May 10, 2011 at 3:36:10 PM EDT

To: faith5239 <faith5239@gmail.com>

Dear Mr. Stridemore,

We did receive your email! I thought that I had responded, so please forgive me! Xxxxx would like to speak with you personally regarding your request. Since you did not share contact information with us, we were unable to reach you. At your convenience, can you please call him at 877-392-XXXX.

Thank you,

Xxxxxxxxx Xxxxxx
www.xxxxxxxxxx.com
910.392.XXXX

From: xxxxxxxxx<xxxxxxx@ec.rr.com>

Subject: Re: SECOND Portrait commission request

Date: May 22, 2011 at 4:51:26 PM EDT

To: faith5239 <faith5239@gmail.com>

Mr. Stridemore,

Just wanting to follow up with you regarding your portrait request. Since we do not have your phone number, we ask that if you are still interested in this project, that you please call Kenny at 877-392-XXXX.

Hope you have had a wonderful weekend and we will look forward to hearing from you soon.

Xxxxxxxx Xxxxxx

www.xxxxxxxxxxx.com

910.392.XXXX

26

From: faith5239 <faith5239@gmail.com>

Subject: Lost dry cleaning item?

Date: April 27, 2011 at 12:20:17 PM EDT

To: customerservice@jimmassey.com

Dear Jim Massey's Customer Service,

I'm a long-time customer who's used your superior dry cleaning services exclusively for years. Frankly no one else can clean a garment like Jim Massey, that's what I always say! Recently, I had an order cleaned at your Norman Bridge Road location as usual (your people are SO NICE there) and only realized today when I needed it, that my Burqa is not in the order. Can you please find it? It's blue, and long and covers the entire body and head, and has a little screen in the front in order to see. Did it possibly get mixed in with another Burqa order? You can tell mine because although you guys do a great job, there's a permanent stain on the front: a small, yellowish stain from a Bear Claw (the pastry, not the animal).

It was in the order that had the burqa (obviously), a men's greyish suit-jacket, and one blue-green mermaid costume with sequins on it, maybe you remember it?

Please check and let me know as soon as possible if you find my burqa. I really need it.

Thanks again very much. I await your reply.

Best regards,
Asiya F. Aleed

From: customerservice@jimmassey.com
Subject: Lost dry cleaning item?
Date: April 28, 2011 at 08:11:12 PM EDT
To: faith5239 <faith5239@gmail.com>

Dear Mrs. Aleed,

We've reviewed your inquiry and find no burqa. Do you have the ticket number? If you can call or email us with it, that would be very helpful. Then we'll have another look, but I will admit we asked the staff working that day and no one recalls an order with a burqa. Maybe the mermaid swam off with it.

Please give us a call and we'll do our best to help.

Have a wonderful day,

XXXX XXXXXX
Office Manager

27

From: faith5239 <faith5239@gmail.com>

Subject: Customer service re hotel room request

Date: March 17, 2011 at 4:57:14 PM EDT

To: customerservice@chumashcasino.com

Dear Chumash Casino Customer Service,

I'll be staying in your fabulous resort for one week starting April 26, and I can't wait! I'll be playing the slot machines, which I LOVE to do once a year, and the best part is this year I'll get to see Michael Bolton! He's fantastic, and besides enjoying your Deluxe King room (the one with no balcony), I can't imagine anything better (besides the service - your housekeeping staff is wonderful - Last

year I got all the little shampoos I needed!).
I can't wait for my vacation at your resort.
I've been saving all year. I do have a very
important request, however: Can you please
have someone trained in the ancient Indian
arts to "Sage" my room to eliminate any Indian
spirits? This is very important; because last
year when I stayed in your fine hotel, I'm sure
I experienced paranormal activity. Is your
resort or casino built on an Indian burial
ground, because that could be the reason? I
understand that a properly trained psychic
can also sage a room, but I just figured
that Indian spirits might better appreciate
an Indian doing the saging. That's just a
suggestion, however - feel free to use either
one!

The important point is that someone must
come in and sage the room to free it of any
spirits. I wouldn't be able to sleep, nor
concentrate on the slot machines, nor enjoy
the vocal stylings of the legendary Michael
Bolton if I'm hearing strange Indian ghosts
bumping about in the night.

Please let me know that you can provide this
service (Since you're an Indian casino, I'm
sure it's not the first time you've had this
request!). When I stayed at your resort last
year, I really felt that your staff went to

great lengths to make my stay thoroughly enjoyable (in spite of the noisy spirits), and I can't wait to enjoy my annual vacation with you once again.

Thanks very much for your prompt attention to this important issue. Please let me know that you can prepare a room for me the way that I've requested. Thank you again, and I'll see you April 26!

Very sincerely,
Andy Bradshaw

From: faith5239 [faith5239@gmail.com]

Sent: Tuesday, March 22, 2011 6:05 PM

To: CustomerService

Subject: SECOND EMAIL FROM A CUSTOMER PLEASE RESPOND

Dear Chumash Casino and Customer Service,

Please can you respond to my very important email below that was sent some weeks ago? I really need to finalize my travel plans and reservations with you -- THANK YOU VERY MUCH, I can't wait to come to your wonderful resort!

Andy

On Wed, Mar 23, 2011 at 7:22 PM,
CustomerService
<CustomerService@chumashcasino.com> wrote:

Hello Andy,

I apologize for the delayed response. I was hoping to have a definitive answer for you before responding. I have contacted the Director of our Hotel to resolve your request. Unfortunately, he is out of the office and has not responded yet. I will respond again as soon as I have a definite answer.

Respectfully,
Chumash Casino Resort
1-800-CHUMASH

From: faith5239 [faith5239@gmail.com]

Sent: Friday, March 25, 2011 8:02 AM

To: CustomerService

Subject: Re: FW: SECOND EMAIL FROM A
CUSTOMER PLEASE RESPOND

Okay, thanks for the update. Please let
me know asap though so I can book my
reservations -- April 26 is coming very
soon, and I can't miss the incredible sounds
of the great Michael Bolton!

Best,
Andy (Big Chamush fan!)

On Fri, Mar 25, 2011 at 2:44 PM,
CustomerService
<CustomerService@chumashcasino.com> wrote:

Hello Andy,

We have arranged for our Spiritual Leader and Cultural Advisor for the Chumash Tribe to come and perform the saging in your hotel room at Chumash Casino Resort.

Please let me know if you would like to be in the room at the time of the saging and we will schedule accordingly. Let me know when you have made your hotel reservations and have a reservation number.

Please feel free to respond if there is anything else I can assist you with. We are looking forward to your visit!
I hope you have a great time and I am sure Michael Bolton will be amazing! :)

Respectfully,
Xxxxx Xxxxxxxx
Chumash Casino Resort
1-800-CHUMASH

From: faith5239 [faith5239@gmail.com]

Sent: Saturday, March 26, 2011 7:53 AM

To: CustomerService

Subject: Re: FW: FW: SECOND EMAIL FROM A CUSTOMER PLEASE RESPOND

Dear Ms. Xxxxxxxx,

WOW -- you are the all-time Queen of good customer service -- I always said that your resort is my favorite vacation destination (very clean rooms!), but this takes it to a whole new level!

I'm SO RELIEVED that a true professional can come to the hotel and address this most important issue. You raise a good question as to whether I want to be present or not. I hadn't thought of that. Which is better? I wonder if the Spirits need to see me, as if to say to them, "I claim this territory!" kind of thing. On the other hand, I hope the Spirits won't be insulted. In that case I wouldn't want them to take it out on me! I'll have to think about that, but I'll give you plenty of notice so you can schedule it just prior to my arrival.

Can you give me a contact email for your boss so that I can sing the praises of your fantastic service? I would really like to do that. I'm so impressed and now I'm even more excited about my trip to see Michael Bolton, all thanks to you!

By the way, is there a charge for the saging ceremony? I don't mind, I just don't know how these things work.

Thanks again SO MUCH for your help with this. I'm truly grateful!

With best regards and gratitude,
Andy

On Fri, Apr 8, 2011 at 1:55 PM,
CustomerService
<CustomerService@chumashcasino.com> wrote:

Hello Andy,

I just wanted to follow up with you to see if you have made your hotel reservations, so we can follow through with providing the saging you requested.

We are looking forward to your visit! Have a great day!

Respectfully,
Xxxxx
Chumash Casino Resort
1-800-CHUMASH

From: faith5239 <faith5239@gmail.com>

Subject: Re: FW: FW: FW: SECOND EMAIL FROM A CUSTOMER PLEASE RESPOND

Date: April 13, 2011 at 1:52:52 PM EDT

To: CustomerService <CustomerService@chumashcasino.com>

Dear Ms. Xxxxxxxx,

Thank you very much for checking on me. I wish I had good news, but last week I tripped over my Springer Spaniel Dexter and sprained my ankle! I was waiting because I thought it would be much better by now, but I think it's actually worse.

I'm very bummed that I have to miss this trip -- but I haven't given up. There's still some time! Once I'm sure I can make it, I'll book the room. Do you think you'll be full? I'll check back next week. Thanks again, you guys are the best!

Regards,
Gimpy Andy

28

From: faith5239 <faith5239@gmail.com>

Subject: Important request regarding my upcoming stay

Date: March 17, 2011 at 7:51:10 PM EDT

To: concierge@hyatt.com

Dear Hyatt Customer Service,

I will be staying with you this June for one week to visit my brother and celebrate my divorce.

I specifically chose your wonderful hotel because I read about how hospitable you've been to the Jehovah's Witnesses each year when they have their convention in town (that and there's no way I'm staying at my brother's – his wife is a piece of work!). Anyway although I'm not a Jehovah's Witness, I am a fairly strict

Catholic (Except for the divorce thing). I've also heard first hand that your staff is among the friendliest anywhere!

In preparation for my week's stay, I have an important request. Can you please stock my room with bottled holy water? I know there are usually bottles of drinking water available, but as I've grown in my walk with God, I've come not only to appreciate Holy water in God's house, but I've also found that drinking it really cleanses my soul through and through! There's no possible way that I could function for an entire week without Holy (drinking) water, especially after the divorce, I need get back on the Holy Mother's good side, if you know what I mean! I would bring the Holy water myself, but airline restrictions on travelling with liquid make it impossible.

I will need two cases for the week. Feel free to put the cost on my bill. I wanted to write you early so that you would have ample time to prepare the cases and have them for my arrival.

I thank you in advance for your wonderful customer service. It's the hallmark of Hyatt. Please confirm as soon as possible, and I look forward to my week at the Sacramento Hyatt!

Best regards,
Jeremy McClain

From: concierge@hyatt.com

Subject: Important request regarding my upcoming stay

Date: March 17, 2011 at 7:51:10 PM EDT

To: faith5239 <faith5239@gmail.com>

Dear Mr. McClain,

Thank you for your very thorough email. I'm sorry to hear about your divorce but very happy that you'll be staying with us in June. Here at Hyatt Sacramento, we do try our very best to ensure that all of our guests have everything they need to be comfortable. I spoke with our Front Desk manager, who discussed your request with our Director of Food and Beverages. He said to let you know that we don't keep Holy Water on property, and would not know where to get any, and even if we did know where to find some, we don't have a courier service so they would have to deliver it. He did suggest, however, that you have the cases of Holy Water delivered to our hotel and we will be more than happy to keep them safe for your arrival.

If you would like to go that route, please let me know so we can be expecting them. I would hate for them to get mixed in with our regular bottled water. Then mail us the cases with "Attention Guest Jeremy McClain" on the address label, along with any special storage instructions ahead of your room assignment, for example if the Holy water requires refrigeration.

We do hope that this will be a viable solution for you. Please feel free to contact me directly should you have any questions and thank you for choosing Hyatt Regency Sacramento, it beats staying at your brother's house!

Regards,
Xxxxxxx Xxxxxx
Hyatt Regency Concierge Associate

From: faith5239 <faith5239@gmail.com>

Subject: Important request regarding my upcoming stay

Date: March 17, 2011 at 7:51:10 PM EDT

To: concierge@hyatt.com

Dear Xxxxxxx at Hyatt Concierge,

If you guys ever have a "Concierge of the year" award, I'm nominating you! I didn't even think about mailing the Holy Water to you, duh!

I'll be in touch in June to remind you that it's coming. You will still be there, in June, right? No reason why you wouldn't, just asking. I would hate to have to explain all of this over again, OR have to stay at my brother's!

Okay well thanks a bunch, you're an angel! (Get it? Holy water, angel, ha!)

Best regards,

Jeremy
A very satisfied customer

29

From: faith5239 <faith5239@gmail.com>

Subject: a group class request

Date: April 27, 2011 at 11:56:11 AM EDT

To: xxxxxx@indyballet.org

Dear Ms. xxxxx,

I'm a nun writing on behalf of my Cloister,
the Sisters of the Holy Sacrament. Our Father
Cantis is having his 75th birthday in June, and
we would like to surprise him with a ballet
recital. So can you teach this group of old
nuns ballet? We don't need to learn anything
fancy; just some basic movements that we can
incorporate into a graceful dance depicting
the Holy Virgin Mary receiving word from the
Arc Angel Gabriel that she will give birth to

the Son of God (that's the Father's favorite story). Can you provide the choreography? Due to our religious beliefs and constraints, we will need to keep our Habits on during the lessons, and obviously the dance movements should be compatible with this. I don't think it will be a problem (As a trial-run, I kicked my ankle up onto the back of a church pew and besides a parishioner looking a bit shocked, I had no problem).

Regarding payment, we are vowed to a life absent of monetary worth, however we've raised enough in donations that we can accept your fee (the Lord provides in all things!)

There will be twelve of us for the lesson, which we would like to schedule for the majority of May. We can come several times a week if necessary, depending upon the cost. Please let me know what you suggest.

Thank you very much for your service and for sharing your gifts with us,

Be Blessed,
Sister Marvin Katherine H. Levine

Me and my Cloister are still waiting...

30

From: faith5239 <faith5239@gmail.com>

Subject: Important question about cows

Date: March 17, 2011 at 7:14:01 PM EDT

To: info@livermoretemple.org

Dear Shiva-Vishnu Temple,

I own a dairy farm in upstate Wisconsin that houses 250 cows, all top milk producers. With the economy so bad, we are sadly forced to close down operations. This leaves me with 250 homeless cows, and I started thinking, hey, would you guys adopt our cows? You might not have room for all of them, but maybe you know other Hindus who would also like to adopt a few? I would transport the them to you, that's no problem. I also have a year's supply of feed, so they won't be much of an expense. You would have to milk them at first, at 5am every morning and evening and at noon. Eventually you could taper off the milking and they would just be normal, lazy cows (no offense!).

So do you want the cows? The cows and I would all be SO HAPPY if you do! Please let me know right away. I'm planning to transport them to you next week and have the truck reserved. Should I bring them to the Temple, or do you have another place?

Thanks very much for probably taking the cows. I know with you they will be so happy and live a long, peaceful life like they deserve.

I look forward to hearing from you soon to confirm the drop-off location.

Best regards and bless you,

Steven R. Welch
Wisconsin Dairy and Farms

On Mon, Mar 28, 2011 at 7:33 PM, Balaji Temple <balajitemple1@gmail.com> wrote:

Dear Steven R Welch,

Thank you so much for the offer.

Unfortunately we are not in a position to accept your offer at this time.

We forwarded your email to temple devotees.

If you need any other help, Please feel free to contact us@ 408-203-XXXX.

Thankyou,
Xxxxxxxxxxxxx

From: faith5239 <faith5239@gmail.com>

Subject: Re: Important question please respond

Date: March 29, 2011 at 2:48:03 PM EDT

To: Balaji Temple <balajitemple1@gmail.com>

Oh, I'm very sorry to hear that you can't take them; I think the cows were getting excited! If any of your temple devotees are interested and think they can help, please have them contact me.

Thank you again very much,
Steve

On Sun, Apr 3, 2011 at 11:54 AM,
Sunita Nag <xxxxxxxxx5@yahoo.com> wrote:

Hi Xxxxxx,
Xxxxxxx Swami told me that you would like
to donate some cows. I am interested in few
if them. Pl. let me know if they are still
avalable. I have a small farm in Hollister.
Also, any number I can call you.

Xxxxxx
408 202 XXXX

From: faith5239 <faith5239@gmail.com>

To: Xxxxxx Xxx <xxxxxxxxx5@yahoo.com>

Sent: Mon, April 4, 2011 7:14:47 AM

Subject: Re: Cows for donation !!

Dear Xxxxxx,

Thank you for contacting me -- my cows will be so happy and I will sleep much better knowing that they're in a good home!

Important question: how many are you interested in taking?

Steve

On Tue, Apr 5, 2011 at 10:11 PM,
Sunita Nag <xxxxxxxxx5@yahoo.com> wrote:

Hi Steve,

Thanks for your reply. I was looking for 2 at this time.. Please, let me know if this will work. Also, may I have the photos pl.

Best regards
Xxxxxx
408 202 XXXX

From: faith5239 <faith5239@gmail.com>

To: Sunita Nag <xxxxxxxxx5@yahoo.com>

Sent: Wed, April 13, 2011 11:13:47 AM

Subject: Re: Cows for donation !!

Dear Xxxxxx,

Thank you so much for your kind offer to adopt
two of my beautiful dairy cows. I've had this
dairy farm for 22 years. I've seen cows come
and go, but this crop of heifers is by far the
best group I've ever had. Not only are they
top milk producers, but they've become like
part of the family. Over the years my wife
has come to name every single one! Eugiene
(our prize milker and named after Princess
Eugiene) can actually walk up the stairs of
our front porch and ring the dinner bell,
she's just the best.

What I'm saying is that after we got your
letter, my wife and I have done a lot of soul
searching about this; the cows have even been
especially restless this week (they're very
sensitive creatures and can smell anxiety)
and we've determined that we just can't
separate the cows. To break them up would be
devastating. We really need to find a home

where all 250 can live together in harmony. Do you have any neighbors with more room?

Thank you again very much for your kindness and caring about our cows. I know they'll all eventually go to a good home.

Best regards,
Steve

From: Xxxxxx Xxx <Xxxxxxxxx5@yahoo.com>

Subject: Re: Cows for donation !!

Date: April 14, 2011 at 11:12:26 PM EDT

To: faith5239 <faith5239@gmail.com>

Dear Steve,

Thank you so much for your reply and concers. I very well understand it, and know how difficult it is to part some one you love. I wish I could had adopted all but cannot.

Thank you so much !!

Best Regards
Xxxxxx

31

EMAILED 3/21/11 VIA THE HN WEBSITE

TO HEBREW NATIONAL

Dear Hebrew National,

I'm not Jewish but I LOVE your hot dogs, they're the best hot dogs in the world! I noticed on your television commercials that you "answer to a higher authority." That's probably why your hot dogs are so good!

As a non-Jew, I'd like to know how you make your hot dogs Kosher. I thought that meant they had to be blessed by a Rabbi. Do you have a Rabbi at your hot dog factory, or by region, or how does it work, exactly? Also, can non-Jews eat Kosher food? I really like your hot dogs, but my wife says we can't eat them because we're not Jewish. Please confirm this.

Thanks very much for answering. Do you also have Kosher buns? That would be a great idea!

Sincerely,
Josh Sikes

conagra_care@conagra.epowercenterdirect.com

to faith5239@gmail.com

3/24/11

Dear Mr. Sikes,

Thank you for your email concerning our Hebrew National Franks.

Your comments are extremely valuable, and they help us make the food you love even better.

Our raw materials must come from animals slaughtered Kosher, which is different from the way animals are slaughtered for non-kosher consumption. The Kashruth requires that the animal be slaughtered in the most humane fashion. For that reason, the slaughter is performed on a fully, conscious animal so that death occurs as quickly and painlessly as possible. The actual kosher slaughter is performed by shochtim (kosher slaughterers) who have been specifically approved by Rabbi Ralbag for that purpose. The shochtim sever the carotid artery and the jugular vein in the neck with a special knife which is free from any nicks or imperfections. This ensures that the blood leaves the carcass as quickly as possible which is significant because the Kashruth forbids kosher observers to consume blood.

A blessing which does include the name of God is made by each slaughterer. The blessing is said over the first animal and the slaughterer has in mind the entire slaughter run he makes for the day. A blessing need not be made for each animal after the first one as this is viewed as taking God's name in vain, which is prohibited.

It is indeed okay for nonjewish persons to consume our products. We are glad to hear that you enjoy them so much.

We will also be sending you coupons via regular mail that will be valid for ninety days. Please allow 1-2 weeks for receipt.

Thanks again for your feedback. We're listening!

Sincerely

Xxxxx
Consumer Affairs Representative
ConAgra Foods
Case: 60041182

1-877-CONAGRA (1-877-266-2472)
www.conagrafoods.com

And they DID send me a lot of great coupons, love these guys!

32

From: faith5239 <faith5239@gmail.com>

Subject: Need help with a question

Date: May 10, 2011 at 3:48:59 PM EDT

To: info@mppc.org

Dear Great Folks at Menlo Park Presbyterian,

I kind of had Pastor Peterson in mind for this letter because I LOVE the Cafe' services, but really it could be for anyone who has some insight (all of you guys!) and wants to share your wisdom.

I'm hoping that you can settle an argument between me and my wife. We've been married for 34 years and have been fairly good

Presbyterians during most of that time and God has blessed us.

Unfortunately I was laid off 4 years ago. I've been looking for a job ever since, but my wife nags me CONSTANTLY - where did you go today, who did you call, what did you do, what's wrong with you, blah, blah, blah - The other day as we were leaving Home Depot (my neighbor keeps driving over my sprinkler heads!) I finally told her that God didn't need her nagging me, and she said, oh yeah? Well if God didn't like it when I nagged you I'm sure He would give me a sign! And EXACTLY then a bird pooped on her shoulder - it was FANTASTIC!!! So I said, Ha! That is SO FUNNY! God has the best sense of humor EVER! And she said that God didn't have a sense of humor, that He is God and as such is very serious, and that's what started the argument that we can't agree on:

Does God have a sense of humor?

I'm not a Bible scholar, but if you had been in the Home Depot parking lot last week you would definitely say yes! So I say that God is AWESOME and He invented humor. My wife (the nag) says that God would not use bird poop to illustrate a point. So we decided to ask an expert. If I'm right, she agrees not to bug me about a job anymore, and if she's right, I have to clean the bird poop off the roof of our tool shed (her idea, now who's the comedian).

So please enlighten us – we can't wait to hear from you!

Thanks a lot, and have a blessed and funny day!

Best regards,
Larry and Helen Dryfuss

From: Xxxxx Xxxxx <churchontherock@aol.com>
Subject: Bird Poop Email Question
Date: March 5, 2012 at 10:33:07 AM EST
To: faith5239@gmail.com

Hi Larry and Helen,

Thank you for the email. I spoke with Pastor Tad regarding it, and he asked me to respond on his behalf.

He wishes you both lots of happiness and peace, and hopes you have been able to settle your disagreement. But, without getting into the details of your argument, he does want you to know, God ABSOLUTELY has a sense of humor!

I hope this helps. Please let us know if we can be of any further assistance. Thanks!

Xxxxx Xxxxx
Church On The Rock
Receptionist
XXXX XXth Ave W
Palmetto, Fl. 34221
941.729.XXXX - Phone
941.723.XXXX - Fax
xxxxx@xxxxfamily.com

33

From: "faith5239" <faith5239@gmail.com>

To: americank9@comcast.net

Sent: Thursday, March 17, 2011 7:48:45 PM

Subject: Need help with my dog

Dear Kathy,

I live in Weymouth with a wonderful six-year old black Labrador Retriever named Bud. I also have two parakeets, Spuds and Sparky, a cat named Ink, and Boris and Natasha, my two ferrets. Three years ago I was taking a walk and found Bud, underweight and disoriented, roaming the streets. He followed me home and ever since then, Bud has been a wonderful and loving addition to our happy home, except for one problem: Bud is a homosexual. Please don't get me wrong, I'm not prejudiced or anything, but I'm a Christian woman and under my roof there are certain rules. It started one morning that first year when I went to change Ink's litter box and found Bud, humping away on Ink, his tail pounding the ground and knocking litter everywhere. Poor Ink just stood there frozen, rhythmically crying out, "Me!-ow!-me-ow!-me!-ow! as Bud did his worst. We've been living with Bud's dirty secret for three years now, but as I grow in my walk with God, me and the other animals just can't take it. I've tried many things to get Bud to see the light. I once found a female black lab around the neighborhood that Bud could have a "date" with, but Bud's not interested. My slutty neighbor Kathleen and her shack-up boyfriend Daniel actually offered up their three-year old Springer Spaniel Daisy, who's in heat. I'm not surprised; she obviously has no idea how inter-racial that is (I don't even want to know what all goes on in that house). The point is that no matter what I try, Bud just refuses to respect that this is a strictly straight household, and no place for his alternative lifestyle. I'm even getting concerned that even worse than being a flaming homosexual, Bud may be a nymphomaniac-homosexual. He can't stop himself. Sometimes he even tries to hump Boris, the male ferret, but he really seems to have a thing for Ink. Last year in desperation

I got him a giant stuffed Panda to hump, but Bud didn't go for it. Once he climbed on but when Ink walked by with his tail in the air, swinging his feline rump around, Bud was back to his old tricks.

I don't know if there are dogs in Heaven, but if there are, I'm pretty sure they're all straight. I had Bud fixed the first year I got him; I don't know what else to do. Since Bud has made it clear that he's not going to reform himself, I feel it's my duty out of love to try and save Bud's soul. I don't know if he needs a Shrink or a Clergy or both. Can you please help me? I'm more than willing to drive to you. And during these sessions, would it be productive for Ink to come as well, to work through any issues or traumas he's sustained during his forced homosexuality? Please let me know as soon as possible. Ink's backside has taken enough.

Sincerely,
Charlene Doan

On Fri, Mar 18, 2011 at 6:56 AM,
<americank9@comcast.net> wrote:

This is a joke right. Humans are gay, dogs
are dominant and for this reason mount other
animals male of female alike and it certainly
doesnt make them homosexual, your dog if its
even real has a bad habit and nothing worse.
I have no desire to watch your dog hump your
cat. If you are serious and need training we
can talk further but at this point it sounds
like a joke.

Good luck!

Xxxx Xxxxxxx
American K-9
774-722-XXXX
www.xxxxxxxxxbreeddogtraining.com

From: faith5239 <faith5239@gmail.com>

Subject: Re: Need help with my dog

Date: March 18, 2011 at 9:28:02 AM EDT

To: americank9@comcast.net

Dear Xxxx,

I'm very sorry you don't believe me. I'm a Christian and I just don't know a lot about homosexuality. I think you could be a little bit more understanding. I contacted you guys because I saw that you are not only qualified animal trainers, but also dog psychologists, and Bud's behavior really bothers me (not to mention Ink).

If you don't want to "watch my dog humping my cat," Maybe you can at least offer some suggestions I can try at home?

Any help would be most sincerely appreciated!

And by the way I really like your website.

Thanks very much,
Charlene

On Fri, Mar 18, 2011 at 9:34 AM,
<americank9@comcast.net> wrote:

Okay if you really have concerns about Bud
and Ink, I think you might want to separate
them. Animals simply do not have the cognitive
reasoning that humans do. They act out of
instinct. If this is a serious problem, maybe
you're not cut out for having pets. If Sparky
and Boris and the gang are behaving according
to your standards, then maybe think about
giving Bud a break.

Good Luck!

Xxxx Xxxxxxx
American K-9
774-722-XXXX
www.xxxxxxxxxbreeddogtraining.com

34

From: faith5239 <faith5239@gmail.com>

Subject: I left something in your cab

Date: March 19, 2011 at 11:20:38 AM EDT

To: southerncabcompany@yahoo.com

Dear Southern Cab Company,

I'm a Hindu and recently traveled in one of
your very nice mini vans on March 2 from
Homewood Suites at 530 Providence Park Drive
East to my favorite Denny's restaurant at 812
S. Beltline Highway at about 9:30 am. Your
driver was very nice and courteous! I left
a nine-pound, gold Buddah in the taxi. Did
you find it? It's about the size of a baby,
sitting cross-legged with a large, round belly
and a big smile. There are no moving parts. I

left it sitting next to me, directly behind the driver's seat. The value is approximately the cost of a bottle of gold-paint, but real gold, not the fake kind. Its value is more sentimental and sacred than anything else.

Please let me know if you found my Buddah. I greatly appreciate your efforts! Your taxi cabs are always very clean and neat and the music is never too loud. I really like that!

Thanks again,
Sanjiv Varshni

From: southerncabcompany@yahoo.com

Subject: Re: I left something in your cab

Date: March 19, 2011 at 1:50:20 PM EDT

To: faith5239 <faith5239@gmail.com>

Thank you for your compliments they are very much appriciated. No we have not had anything turned in for the past month

35

Dear Ritz Carlton Naples,

Recently I visited your hotel and performed a Haitian ritual cleansing for one of your guests. This is a highly involved spiritual process, and requires a lot of concentration and also a lot of stuff. Afterwards, I went through the lobby and used your downstairs restroom (near the pool and pool cafe), where I unfortunately left my cleansing kit. Did you find it? It would have been on the counter by the sink closest to the door. All of the items should be together in the kit, but just in case you find some randomly, following is a list of the items:

One chicken claw

One pickled chicken's beak

Four feathers from a black crow in a blue drawstring bag

One multi-colored cotton and silk priest's robe, size large

Matches (small box)

Incense sticks (in a silver tin)

2-dram vile of Mambo Michele's "Day-in-Court" voodoo ritual oil

One green cat candle

One goat's milk voodoo spiritual soap-on-a-rope

One bottle of "4-thieves" vinegar

Anti-hex batch liquid

Erzulie's War Water, small

One tooth (mine, not part of kit)

I really hope you found my kit. Thanks for looking. Please let me know.

Sincerely,
Rev. Sagbo Zaka

From: faith5239 [mailto:faith5239@gmail.com]

Sent: Saturday, April 02, 2011 11:54 AM

To: RC, Naples Beach Guest Services

Subject: SECOND REQUEST PLEASE RESPOND

Fwd: Left something important in your hotel

Dear Ritz Carlton Naples,

I'm highly disappointed and frustrated that you did not respond to my rather urgent email concerning my having left my Haitian Ritual Cleansing Kit in one of your hotel bathrooms. This kit is highly important to me, took a long time to complete and is worth considerable value to me.

In my initial letter below, I detailed where I left it on Sunday, March 20, and also mentioned that the kit may have been gone through and various pieces may be found around the property, so I list the items in the kit in the hope that if you don't find the entire kit in tact, that at least if you happen to find a chicken claw or tooth laying around, you'll know it's mine and contact me.

Now, because you have failed to respond in a timely manner, my Cleansing Kit and its contents are very likely lost or stolen, thanks to you. I'm extremely saddened by this and disappointed in your lack of concern for your guests.

I would sincerely like a response from you, either that you DID find the kit or some of its contents and that it's just sitting in your lost and found (did you check??) or, at least an apology for aiding in its being lost since you didn't see fit to address the issue when I originally wrote you.

Thank you again, and please do acknowledge promptly.

Best regards,
H.P. Ramtha Zibadeau

From: RC, Naples Beach Guest Services
<rc.rswrz.servidyne@ritzcarlton.com>

Date: Mon, Apr 11, 2011 at 12:39 PM

Subject: FW: SECOND REQUEST PLEASE RESPOND
Fwd: Left something important in your hotel

To: faith5239@gmail.com

Dear Sir/Madame,

Our Lost and Found Department has been contacted and we are actively looking for the below kit.

Unfortunately, we have not been successful in recovering the lost items.

Please provide us with your telephone number as well so we may contact you if those items are found.

Warmest regards,

Xxxxxxx Xxxxx
Guest Relations
The Ritz-Carlton, Naples
280 Vanderbilt Beach Rd.
Naples FL 34108
Ph # 239-598-XXXX
e-mail Xxxxxxx.xxxxx@ritzcarlton.com

36

EMAILED 3/17/11

Xxxxx@mannequinmannequins.com

MannequinMannequins.com

Dear Xxxxx,

I've just recently taken over the largest privately-owned Hebrew store chain in greater Miami, Ft. Lauderdale and Boca Raton. As part of our major renovation I need 200 Jewish mannequins. I've searched everywhere, and I'm horrified as to the lack of Jewish representation in the mannequin industry. You claim to have the largest selection of mannequins "anywhere in the U.S.," and yet your Ethnic section only has a few African-American women and one Asian guy. Where are the Jews? I need a mix: mostly straight

Jewish, about 25% Orthodox and 10% Hasidic Jew complete with Peyos (those funny curls on the side of the men's heads).

Please let me know a price on this asap, shipping time, etc.

Thanks very much,

Samuel Lochowitz
Lochowitz & Sons Clothiers, Inc.

I guess they're really backed up with orders…

37

http://www.scientology-losangeles.org/
contact.html

EMAILED 4/23/11 RE THE CHURCH OF SCIENTOLOGY
SUBMISSION FORM:

Dear Church of Scientology,

Due to a job transfer, my family and I are
relocating to Los Angeles, where we'll be
looking for a new church. We're Baptists, but
since I told her about the move my wife has
become OBSESSED with your church – she insists
that if we attend your Sunday services and
join your church, we will rub elbows with the
Cruises and Travoltas and that our daughter
Sophie will attend Scientology school with
Surie Cruise and we'll all become the best of
friends. She's driving me nuts!

So can you PLEASE settle this disagreement between us by answering the following: if we attend your church, will we meet famous people, will our daughter meet famous children, does John Travolta perform in Scientology talent shows or give complimentary dance lessons (sorry for that one!) and finally, does being a Scientologist give you a vote with the American Academy of Arts and Sciences (this is where my crazy wife thinks the "Science" part of your name comes from).

Seriously, if you can confirm any of this or better yet, deny it, my wife promises to abide by whatever answers you send and finally give me some peace!

Thank you very much for the clarification,
David (and Jeannie) Simmons

On Tue, Apr 26, 2011 at 3:26 PM, wrote:

Hi David,

Your email was great. Though I can't confirm or deny that you will ever run into any famous people if you join the Church of Scientology, I also cannot confirm or deny you won't run into any famous people just walking around in LA. I can understand your wife's desire to rub noses with successful, intelligent people, and if you applied the Technology of Scientology you would be come more able and thus, well, anything is possible once you get to that point!

If you are still in the area, I would love to give you a tour of our new building in Ybor Square. You can get some more information on Scientology, what it is, how it helps people etc..

And, of course, it will help your wife "get it out of her system."

You can call me on my cell 727-XXX-XXXX or email me back to set up a time for a tour.

Sincerely,
Xxxxx Xxxxxx

From: "faith5239@gmail.com"

Sent: Sunday, April 24, 2011 5:15 PM

Subject: Re: Your Request

Hi Xxxxx,

Thanks so much for the information, my wife is now more obsessed than ever. We'd love to take a tour (Actually, my wife insists on it) and last night over dinner I was informed that we're taking dance lessons in case we run into Travolta. Great.

But seriously, your response was so great in helping us to get excited about our move and thinking about the possibilities of making new "Science" friends, so thank you for that!

We're not in Los Angeles yet, but when we get there, I'll give you a call!

Thanks again and best regards,
David

From: <losangeles@scientology.net>
Subject: Regarding the email on Scientology
Date: June 4, 2011 at 1:07:47 AM EDT
To: <faith5239@gmail.com>

Dear David,

Hi there. My name is Xxxxx and I work at the Church of Scientology in LA. How are you?

I just read your email on moving to LA and your wife being "obsessed" with our church. :)

Well I don't think you'll see Tom Cruise or John Travolta in here, but if your wife still really wants to find out about Scientology let her know that she's more than welcome to come in for a tour of our Information Center. I hope this helps!

Sincerely,
Xxxxx Xxxxxxx
Church of Scientology
4810 Sunset Blvd.
Los Angeles, CA 90027
Sent: 3 June 2011 14:52

This was the beginning of about 20 more emails. These guys are persistent!

38

From: faith5239 <faith5239@gmail.com>

Subject: Important question re coming to visit

Date: March 17, 2011 at 7:41:48 PM EDT

To: winklerbaptistchurch@embarqmail.com

Dear Pastor Xxxxxxx,

I'm visiting Ft. Myers next week and look forward to attending your 11am Sunday service. The issue is that I have severe flatulence and need certain accommodations.

Severe flatulence due to IBS (Irritable Bowel Syndrome) is a serious medical condition and not a joke. I grow tired of having to explain this, but I have to in order to avoid persecution and ridicule. You have no idea what it's like to sit in church and hear people whisper, "Oh my gosh, what is that smell?!" just before they move to another pew. I love the Lord and want to worship just like everybody else!

Normally it's not a problem, as I've attended the same church for the last 25 years and I think everyone here has just gotten used to it. Next week, however I have to be in Ft. Myers for a funeral, and I never miss Sunday service.

So to prepare for my visit, can you please provide the following: if I can sit near an outlet, please provide a stand-alone, three-speed fan with "hi" speed. If I can't be near an outlet, please provide a hand-fan, or let me know so I can bring one. Also, I will bring nose-plugs for everyone sitting within a 10-foot radius. I will therefore need to know approximately how many people that might be, and if you'd be able to pass the nose-plugs out to that area before service begins.

If you could assist me in this, I would truly appreciate it. God helps those who help themselves.

I need to order the nose-plugs within the next
24 hours to get the bulk-rate discount, so if
you could respond as soon as possible I would
be very grateful.

Thank you again, and may God bless you,

Myra Barnes
Sandusky, Ohio

From: winklerbaptistchurch@embarqmail.com
Subject: Important question re coming to visit
Date: March 18, 2011 at 8:22:39 AM EDT
To: faith5239 <faith5239@gmail.com>

Dear Mrs. Barnes,

Thank you for your frank and honest email. It was "refreshing." (A little flatulence humor). Don't worry about any special accommodations for our parishioners. If you feel uncomfortable sitting with the general assembly, we have a very comfortable room to the side of the worship hall that we usually use for family members to sit privately while still being able to see and hear funeral services. That's a very private place. If you wish to sit in there, just tell any usher your name and that your wish to observe the service from the "Family Room."

I hope this helps alleviate your concerns. We look forward to welcoming you to our Winkler Baptist family during your stay. In the meantime don't hesitate to contact us with any other concerns.

May the Lord bless you,
Pastor Xxxxxxx

39

Guest needs assistance

faith5239 faith5239@gmail.com

Saturday, April 23, 2011 9:54:03 AM

Dear Calvary Church,

Next month I'll be visiting the beautiful town of Westlake Village, where I enjoy hiking in your wonderful hills, eating some of the best food around and generally just enjoying the weather. I don't like to miss church, however, so I'm coming to your church and there's a small matter that I need your assistance with prior to my arrival. I look exactly like George W. Bush, as in, the 43rd President of the United States. I don't mean that I resemble him, I'm the spitting image. Everywhere I go, I get stopped and asked to sign autographs; some people say nice things and want a photo and others tell me what a jerk I am. You might think it's fun for me, but on the contrary it's quite a disability!

So as a result of my uncanny likeness to "W" I've gotten used to having to make certain arrangements for my security when traveling. To that end, are you able to allow me to enter and exit your Sunday service through a side or back entrance, and can you provide any security to sit beside me during services? If not, can you assist me in arranging for such service? I would also be willing to sit in a mourning room or similar where there is audio feed of the sermon. I hate to miss out on the praise and worship portions, but believe me, this is just as much for your convenience as it is mine – do you have any idea how much pandemonium it will cause if I, George W. Bush (or so people will think) just walk right into your Sunday Worship Service? No one would pay attention to anything but me! I promise, I've learned from experience! So please let me know the best way to attend your services. I would prefer your 11am but of course I'm flexible! Thank you very much for your attention to this important matter.

Best regards,
Warren Stevenson

p.s. Happy Easter!

From: Steve Day <steved@calvarycc.org>

Subject: How Can I Help?

Date: May 2, 2011 at 1:16:52 PM EDT

To: faith5239@gmail.com

Good Morning Mr. Stevenson,

When it comes to your experience at Calvary, If I can help you in any way, please feel free to give me a call. Around here, we're used to dealing with celebrities, real or otherwise, so I'm sure we can accommodate you.

Blessings,
Xxxxx

--

Pastor Xxxxxx X. Xxx
General Ministry Oversight
Care/Support/Recovery
Adult Ministries
Missions
Calvary Community Church
Westlake Village, Ca
818-575-XXXX
www.calvarycc.org
"To Live and Love Like Jesus"

From: faith5239 <faith5239@gmail.com>

Subject: Re: How Can I Help?

Date: May 10, 2011 at 2:57:29 PM EDT

To: Xxxxx Xxx <Xxxxxx@calvarycc.org>

Dear Pastor Xxxxx,

So sorry for the delayed response; I thought I'd sent you one already. Thank you so much for your accessibility and willingness to help! You just have NO IDEA how inconvenient it is at times to look like G.W. Bush. In the past I considered growing a beard or growing my hair long, but I just don't like those things, so why should I?

At any rate, thank you again and when my travel plans are solidified, I'll contact you to discuss any options. I'm looking forward to attending your service!

God Bless,
Warren

40

From: faith5239 [mailto:faith5239@gmail.com]

Sent: Thursday, March 17, 2011 7:46 PM

To: Xxx Xxxx

Subject: Important question re coming to visit

Dear Pastor Xxxx,

On March 25th I'll be coming to Ft. Myers to stay with my sister for a month, and get away from the freezing cold of Michigan! At home, I regularly attend church services, and my faith is incredibly important to me. My sister is a regular parishioner in your church, and while visiting I would like to attend services with her every Sunday. My home church knows me well, so I'm very comfortable there, but since I'll be a visitor, I'd like to let you know that I'm blind, and I will be attending services with my guide horse, Daisy.

If you're not familiar with guide horses, Daisy is a miniature horse, about the size of a German Shepherd, and comes from a wonderful organization called the Guide Horse Foundation. There are actually about 150,000 guide horses in the United States, but I've yet to run into any of them besides Daisy! (If you want, you can check them out at: http://www.guidehorse. org/art_tonto_philly_inq.htm).

Anyway, Daisy is a wonderful horse, and won't be any problem. I've had her for three years, so we're really used to each other, and so far, she's been almost perfectly housebroken. If she needs to potty, she scratches her hoof on the floor, and then I would have to take her outside to do her business. Because of this, we should sit on the isle, and don't worry – she's fitted with four, specially adapted baby shoes so that she doesn't scratch up the floor! She's really quite something to see – a tiny horse wearing shoes (Except sadly, I can't see her). Also we would need to be directed to some small patch of grass of your choosing, perhaps a spot that needs fertilizing. Daisy only had an accident twice, and once wasn't her fault because someone fed her cupcakes at a church social and she got a horrible stomach ache. If you want, I could put a very small bag around her tail to catch any "business," and just let her do her thing. Either way is fine with Daisy, we just need to know.

Besides that and maybe a small bucket of water would be nice after the service, Daisy and I won't be any trouble. But since people are sometimes surprised by a guide horse, I like to let you know ahead of time. Daisy and I would see you for four Sundays at the second service; I think it's at 10:30.

Please confirm that this is okay. Daisy and I can't wait to come and worship with you and your wonderful church. I know your church is wonderful because my sister told me so, and she's VERY particular.

Thanks so much, and I look forward to hearing from you soon.

With warm regards,
Ellie May Burkett

On Tue, Mar 22, 2011 at 11:21 AM,
Xxx Xxxx <xxx@riversidechurch.org> wrote:

Ellie May,

We are so glad that you are coming to Riverside
and I hope it will be a great experience for
you while you are here. You do whatever is
best for you and Daisy and we will adjust!

Now, I have to warn you. This Sunday, March
27, it will be one service at 10:30 and it
will be packed with people. It's a celebration
of what God has done through our recent Heaven
series. After the service we will be having
a potluck, games, inflatables and hay rides
for the kids, so don't be surprised if people
think your miniature pony is one of the
"attractions." I just hope all the noise and
people won't startle Daisy.

Would you be okay if I announced you and Daisy
so that people were aware and sensitive to you
all? I won't embarrass you. I thought it might
be good since you will be here for the next
few weeks as well. It's not every day that you
have a tiny horse in our sanctuary J

Let me know. Thanks so much and I look forward
to connecting with you.

Xxx Xxxx
Senior Pastor
Riverside Church
239-XXX-XXXX
www.riversidechurch.org

From: faith5239 [mailto:faith5239@gmail.com]

Sent: Wednesday, March 23, 2011 3:32 PM

To: Xxx Xxxx

Subject: Re: Important question re coming to visit

Dear Pastor Xxxx,

Thank you SO MUCH -- you have no idea how challenging it can be sometimes to arrange things for Daisy and me -- when people meet her, they love her to pieces, but prior to that she's sometimes a tough sell. Daisy and I are looking forward to worshiping with you. We'll arrive a bit early just to give Daisy a look around (My sister will probably be with me but she's a bit moody so you never know).

Anyway, thanks so much again for all of your help and understanding. What a great church!

With much love and gratitude,
Ellie May and Daisy

On Wed, Mar 23, 2011 at 4:58 PM,
Xxx Xxxx <xxx@riversidechurch.org> wrote:

We look forward to meeting you and Daisy on Sunday.

Xxx Xxxx
Senior Pastor
Riverside Church
239-XXX-XXXX
www.riversidechurch.org

From: faith5239 <faith5239@gmail.com>

Subject: Re: Important question re coming to visit

Date: March 25, 2011 at 11:10:16 AM EDT

To: Bob Reed <xxx@riversidechurch.org>

Dear Pastor Xxxx,

Bad news -- Daisy has hoof fungus -- Obviously I couldn't see it, but horse handler Bud did and said it's pretty bad. She's not in pain or anything, but she has to get some treatment and proper medication so we have to change our travel plans. I had the trailer all ready to go for yesterday and Bud put the cabash on our plans. I'll most likely be down in the summer instead, so I'll send you guys a note just prior. Have a great weekend and thanks for everything. I have a blind friend in Bonita I'm going to tell her about your church. You guys are terrific.

Thanks again for everything. I'll see you in the summer!

God bless,
Ellie May and Daisy (with hoof fungus) :(

41

EMAILED TO JAMES MADISON UNIVERSITY VIA
WEBSITE CONTACT FORM:

4/23/11

http://www.jmu.edu/philrel/rel/contact.html

xxxxxxxx@jmu.edu

Dear Dr. Xxxxxxx and the Department of
Philosophy and Religion,

On behalf of the Temple of the Jedi Order, I wish
to thank you for your invitation to speak with
regards to your REL 370 course on "Mysticism,"
and as you indicated, also possibly with your
REL 380, "Contemporary Theologies" course.

I'm pleased to accept your invitation, and
have only a few additional questions.

As you are no doubt aware, the study of the Jedi are steeped in ancient philosophies and root themselves in the tension between light and dark. As Obi Wan Kenobi said, "The force is all around us, it binds us together." So we of different faiths are bound together in one universe. In the words of the great Yoda, "Much to learn, have you." And so we learn through study and the sharing of great wisdom, as you do at your wonderful University.

In anticipation of my visit, I have only a few questions. Can your administration offer any guidance as to a quiet place to stay while I'm there? Do you have a mediation room or temple? Can you recommend a good dry cleaner for my Ceremonial Priest's robe? Is there any problem with my bringing my light saber to the speech? Do you think some of the students would want to try it?

I thank you very kindly for your gracious hospitality and for the opportunity for the Jedi to instruct your young scholars in the ways of The Force.

I will look forward to your response, and will see you on June 10 at 8:30am at your office as discussed.

MTFBWY,

Master Neaj Palago, Abrahamic Order
Temple of the Jedi Order
http://templeofthejediorder.org/

From: xxxxxxxx@jmu.edu

Subject: Re: Important question re coming to visit

Date: March 25, 2011 at 11:10:16 AM EDT

To: faith5239 <faith5239@gmail.com>

Dear Master Paggo,

I have no such record of the discussion you reference nor any speaking engagement about the Jedi on any date. I have no idea who you spoke to but I'm truly sorry for any confusion. We have no speaking event planned for June 10 or any other date for this topic so please don't plan any travel.

Again I'm very sorry for whatever mix-up may have occurred.

Sincerely,
Dr. Xxxxxxx

42

From: faith5239 <faith5239@gmail.com>

Subject: Important religious question -
please respond

Date: March 17, 2011 at 7:52:55 PM EDT

To: xxxxxx@fpcbonita.org

Dear Rev. Xxxxx,

I was raised Presbyterian and live in Bonita.
I attended your church for a long time but
since my hip surgery two years ago, I'm not
able to get around as much. I'm writing to
you with a question that no one else has been
able to answer. My husband Frank (of 34 years)
has heart disease and although he's had three
by-passes the doctors are certain that he's
not going to live much longer. In fact, he

could die any time now. That's not what I'm writing about, however. That is to say I've already come to peace with all of that, and Frank has too.

Six years ago, Frank went into kidney failure and I gave him one of my kidneys. Now that Frank's dying, can I have my kidney back? Is there anything non-Presbyterian about that? The kidney is still perfectly fine, and it was mine, so I see no reason why I can't have it back. I already know I have to go through several authorities for this, which I've already started, but I'm writing you to get an okay from the Highest Authority! So is this okay? Ethically speaking?

Thanks for your input very soon. Frank could go any time and I would need to get the kidney while it's still fresh.

Best to you and God Bless,

Sincerely,
Hazel Bartlett

From: "Xxxx Xxxxx" <xxxxxx@fpcbonita.org>
Subject: RE: Important religious question - please respond
Date: March 18, 2011 at 10:15:21 AM EDT
To: "'faith5239'" <faith5239@gmail.com>

Dear Hazel,

I see no moral problems with you seeking to have a "reverse transplant" of your own kidney on your husband's death. This does not involve any ethical complications from a Christian or biblical standpoint. I pray that the Lord will help Frank through his final days with relief of pain and inner peace, and also help you in what you'll be facing.

Yours in Christ,
Pastor Xxxx Xxxxx

43

From: faith5239 <faith5239@gmail.com>

Subject: Journalist question for upcoming article-please respond asap

Date: March 17, 2011 at 8:06:22 PM EDT

To: xxxx.xxxxx@macys.com

Cc: xxx.xxxxxxxxx@macys.com

Dear Ms. Xxxxx,

I'm writing an article for *Jewish Business Magazine* about the severe lack of Jewish mannequins in America's department stores. In my research, Macy's is among the leading chains that seem to have no presence of Jewish mannequins of any kind: no straight Jews, no Orthodox and no Hasidic Jews with Peyos (those funny curls on the side of the men's heads).

According to the U.S. Census Bureau, there are over 6 million Jewish Americans. As a consumer group, the purchasing power of the Jewish American population is considerable. Yet as a company that prides itself on diversity, a total of zero Jewish mannequins exist in Macy's stores. Can you please comment on this? Macy's' policy is crucial to the accuracy of the story.

(Due to submission deadlines this article is time-sensitive so please respond asap).

Thank you,

Stacey Lubbock,
For *Jewish Business Magazine*

From: faith5239 <faith5239@gmail.com>

Subject: Journalist question for upcoming article-please respond asap

Date: March 23, 2011 at 7:42:16 PM EDT

To: Xxxxxxx@macys.com

Cc: xxxxxx@macys.com

Dear Ms. Xxxx and Mr. Xxxxx,

Can you please respond to my email below sent on 3/17/11? I'm disappointed that Macy's does not consider it necessary to reply to inquiries. I'm not only a journalist but also a customer, and from a customer service standpoint, it's good policy to send a reply. I would also greatly appreciate it, as I delayed this feature in order to try and include your policy on this important issue. Millions of Jewish Americans would be interested to know why you don't represent this important purchasing group in your displays. It also wouldn't look very good in my article to have to leave this question unanswered, as though you don't have any concern for your Jewish customers. A reply is best for the story in order to properly represent your stance on this.

I eagerly await to hear from you, and thank
you very much for your time on this important
matter. Please see my original email below.

Thanks again,
Stacey Lubbock

On Wed, Mar 23, 2011 at 9:29 AM, <xxxxxxxxx@ macys.com> wrote:

Mr. Lubbock: I am very sorry we didn't respond sooner.

Mannequins are inanimate objects and, as such, do not practice any religion. Our goal is to display the fashions we offer, not to draw attention to the mannequin itself.

Thanks for providing us the opportunity to comment. --XXX

Xxx Xxxxxx * SVP, Corporate Communications & External Affairs * Macy's, Inc.

Ñ XXXX West Seventh Street, Cincinnati, OH 45202 (

513-579-XXXX 7 513-579-XXXX
* XXXXXXXXX@macys.com

From: faith5239 <faith5239@gmail.com>

Subject: Re: SECOND EMAIL PLEASE RESPOND

Date: March 23, 2011 at 2:45:16 PM EDT

To: xxx.xxxxxxxxx@macys.com

Dear Mr. Xxxxxxxxx,

Thank you very much for your prompt reply; I truly do appreciate it. While I understand your point about mannequins not having a religion, I wasn't actually referring to Jews as a religious group, but rather as a race, just as there are black people and Chinese people and Indian people, Jews are race of people from Israel, who also happen to comprise a religious group. So it is in this manner that I ask why you don't have mannequins that represent the important Jewish segment of your customers, just as you have male and female mannequins, African-American mannequins, and so on. Meaning, particularly in areas of the country that represent high Jewish populations, such as Dearborn, MI; Boca Raton, FL; or Palm Beach, FL, for example, you could have a combination of regular Jewish mannequins, and some Hasidic Jewish mannequins, with the curls on the sides of their heads. I hope this better explains my inquiry.

Can you please expand on your answer? It would better clarify your position on the issue as I present it in the article.

Thank you very much,
Stacey Lubbock

44

From: faith5239 <faith5239@gmail.com>

Subject: Important product question

Date: March 17, 2011 at 4:53:07 PM EDT

To: Info@GoodEarthFoods.com

Dear Good Earth Foods,

I'm a loyal customer of five years. I shop at your store and nowhere else because your products are so pure and superior in every way. Recently I started buying your Noni juice, and I drink a lot of it, at least five times a day (it's really good!). Since I started drinking it, something remarkable has happened. Your Noni juice gives me healing powers. I can't say it's HUGE powers, like I haven't made any one walk or anything, but I CAN cure my dog

Warren's headaches. Warren is a four-year-old black Labrador and for the last two years he's been plagued with debilitating headaches. After I drink a whole bottle of Noni, I lay hands on him and he's cured! Within minutes he's up jumping around and wagging his tail, knocking over the planters just like he used to when he was a puppy! I know it's the juice, because it only works after I've had it, and nothing else will do the trick. I've noticed I have to keep a steady supply of it in my system, though, or the healing powers tend to fade.

This is really so remarkable, and I wanted to tell you first, how FANTASTIC that is, how your Noni juice has changed our lives, and how now that I know that your Noni juice is the secret, I'd like to try an experiment and up my intake of it to a FULL CASE A DAY. I figure that way, I can heal more ailments for Warren, like his canine arthritis, or even move on to people! I just don't know the right amount of your wonderful Noni juice to take that will tip the scales.

So thank you for this miracle drink! Please don't stop making it. Have you heard of this phenomenon before with the Noni juice? Have other people written to you with the same thing? Maybe we should all get together and make a commercial for you, like Jared did with Subway when he lost all that weight. We could all talk about the incredible healing powers of Noni juice!

Please let me know if you would like me to make a testimony for you. Or at least if I can order this juice by the case. That's really why I'm writing but the testimony would be free from me, as a thank you.

Thanks again and please write soon if I can have the Noni juice by the case.

Cheers, and may the Noni juice be with you,
Cheryl Brock

p.s. If you need me to lay hands on anyone in the Good Earth Foods Company, I'm more than happy to. Just please provide the Noni juice prior to my visit for optimal healing powers

From: xxxxgoodearthfoods.com
Subject: Re: Important product question
Date: March 18, 2011 at 10:12:23 AM EDT
To: faith5239 <faith5239@gmail.com>

Wow Cheryl, That is really cool! So far you are the first we have heard of anybody experiencing this kind of reaction. I would suggest approaching the specific Good Earth store you originally make your purchases at to find out if a case qty. is a possibility. Thanks so much for sharing this experience. We can't do commercials any time soon but may I use your testimony in our weekly email blast? Go Warren!

Xxxx (Good Earth)

From: faith5239 <faith5239@gmail.com>
Subject: Re: Important product question
Date: March 18, 2011 at 11:44:57 AM EDT
To: xxxx@goodearthfoods.com

Thanks for the enthusiasm, Xxxx – I always knew I liked Good Earth stores because of its great people! If I make any progress with the cases, I'll let you know!

Thanks again,
Cheryl (and a headache-free Warren)

"He puzzled and puzzled till
his puzzler was sore.

Then the Grinch thought of
something he hadn't before.

Maybe Christmas, he thought,
doesn't come from a store.

Maybe Christmas, perhaps,
means a little bit more!

And what happened then? Well,
in Whoville they say

That the Grinch's small heart
grew three sizes that day!

And then the true meaning of
Christmas came through,

And the Grinch found the strength
of ten Grinches, plus two!"

- *How the Grinch Stole
Christmas,* by Dr. Seuss

The End...?

For more books, products,
courses & other cool stuff

by Stephanie Maier

visit:

www.FreedomDiner.us

www.ingramcontent.com/pod-product-compliance
Lightning Source LLC
Chambersburg PA
CBHW072342090426
42741CB00012B/2893